LITERARY COCKTAIL

LITERARY COCKTAIL
AN ANTHOLOGY

EDITED BY

NICOLE EISENBRAUN
LAURA GERKIN
ABIGAIL GOODWIN
LANI HANSON
CORA MCKNIGHT
ROSAMOND THALKEN

ISBN: 978-1-60962-101-8

Managing Editor: Rosamond Thalken
Acquisitions Editor: Abigail Goodwin
Copy Editor: Nicole Eisenbraun
Marketing Director: Laura Gerkin
Production Director: Cora McKnight
Design Director: Lani Hanson

FOR DR. BEV AND PAUL.
WITHOUT YOU, NONE OF THIS
WOULD HAVE BEEN POSSIBLE.
THANK YOU.

TABLE OF CONTENTS

9 INTRODUCTION

11 OSCAR WILDE
13 THE PICTURE OF DORIAN GRAY (PREFACE)
14 PANTHEA

21 DOROTHY PARKER
23 MEN: A HATE SONG
25 SUCH A PRETTY LITTLE PICTURE
33 REFORMERS: A HYMN OF HATE

37 F. SCOTT FITZGERALD
39 THE BEAUTIFUL AND DAMNED (EXCERPT)
45 JEMINA, THE MOUNTAIN GIRL
50 THE CUT-GLASS BOWL (EXCERPT)

55 EDGAR ALLAN POE
57 LIFE IN DEATH
61 SPIRITS OF THE DEAD
62 A DREAM WITHIN A DREAM
63 MYSTIFICATION

71 JAMES JOYCE
73 GAS FROM A BURNER
76 DUBLINERS: A LITTLE CLOUD
85 THE HOLY OFFICE

89 O. HENRY
91 THE MURDERER
93 NOTHING TO SAY
94 DROP A TEAR IN THIS SLOT

97 AUTHOR BIOGRAPHIES

101 APPENDIX

INTRODUCTION

"Only one? Come on. Just one more sip!" his friend pressed.
"I've got to finish this story first."
"Maybe it'll help you loosen up. Just try it."

And he did. That was the end of it; a little peer pressure and alcohol became his writing crutch, the period at the end of his sentence, the ellipses that kept him wanting more. Soon enough, it was all he had. The words he couldn't quite say from his own lips written in black on a white piece of paper like a tragedy smacking an innocent bystander…and from that tragedy, magic ignited, fire to alcohol, and set the reading world ablaze.

Just shortly before the Prohibition in America, we saw a world of flourishing authors. To the public eye, these people were creative, witty, and full of ideas. They had lists of statements to make and thoughtful questions to pose. They were making an effort, and people were buying into it. The result was less than desirable, and even deadly, for a few of these authors, but not because they were solely writers. The writing was what they clung to in the worst of times, but the booze…the booze was what they used, or rather abused, to help them get it down on paper.

Whether it's true today or a misplaced statement from ancient times, great authors have always had a tendency to rely on alcohol. Once one chooses to use it in their writing journey, it becomes a large part of their lives. This decision has been made for centuries, and for better or worse, some of the world's best pieces of writing have derived from it. This decision also led to many deaths of writers, taking them from the world that had only just begun loving their works.

In an attempt to showcase the works driven by the effects of alcohol, we have selected an array of thrilling, comedic, and sometimes creepy stories and poems from six of the most well-known alcoholic authors in history. Likely under the influence of alcohol, James Joyce, Edgar Allan Poe, O. Henry, F. Scott Fitzgerald, Dorothy Parker, and Oscar Wilde each produced numerous works. We've chosen some of the best, and only part of the time were some of us enjoying our favorite alcoholic beverages.

So please sit down, lean back, take a sip, and enjoy.

OSCAR WILDE

*"Work is the curse
of the drinking classes."*

THE PICTURE OF DORIAN GRAY (PREFACE)

The artist is the creator of beautiful things. To reveal art and conceal the artist is art's aim. The critic is he who can translate into another manner or a new material his impression of beautiful things.

The highest as the lowest form of criticism is a mode of autobiography. Those who find ugly meanings in beautiful things are corrupt without being charming. This is a fault.

Those who find beautiful meanings in beautiful things are the cultivated. For these there is hope. They are the elect to whom beautiful things mean only beauty.

There is no such thing as a moral or an immoral book. Books are well written, or badly written. That is all.

The nineteenth century dislike of realism is the rage of Caliban seeing his own face in a glass.

The nineteenth century dislike of romanticism is the rage of Caliban not seeing his own face in a glass. The moral life of man forms part of the subject-matter of the artist, but the morality of art consists in the perfect use of an imperfect medium. No artist desires to prove anything. Even things that are true can be proved. No artist has ethical sympathies. An ethical sympathy in an artist is an unpardonable mannerism of style. No artist is ever morbid. The artist can express everything. Thought and language are to the artist instruments of an art. Vice and virtue are to the artist materials for an art. From the point of view of form, the type of all the arts is the art of the musician. From the point of view of feeling, the actor's craft is the type. All art is at once surface and symbol. Those who go beneath the surface do so at their peril. Those who read the symbol do so at their peril. It is the spectator, and not life, that art really mirrors. Diversity of opinion about a work of art shows that the work is new, complex, and vital. When critics disagree, the artist is in accord with himself. We can forgive a man for making a useful thing as long as he does not admire it. The only excuse for making a useless thing is that one admires it intensely.

PANTHEA

Nay, let us walk from fire unto fire,
  From passionate pain to deadlier delight,—
I am too young to live without desire,
  Too young art thou to waste this summer night
Asking those idle questions which of old
Man sought of seer and oracle, and no reply was told.

For, sweet, to feel is better than to know,
  And wisdom is a childless heritage,
One pulse of passion—youth's first fiery glow,—
  Are worth the hoarded proverbs of the sage:
Vex not thy soul with dead philosophy,
Have we not lips to kiss with, hearts to love, and eyes to see!

Dost thou not hear the murmuring nightingale
  Like water bubbling from a silver jar,
So soft she sings the envious moon is pale,
  That high in heaven she is hung so far
She cannot hear that love-enraptured tune,—
Mark how she wreathes each horn with mist, yon late and labouring moon.

White lilies, in whose cups the gold bees dream,
  The fallen snow of petals where the breeze
Scatters the chestnut blossom, or the gleam
  Of boyish limbs in water,—are not these
Enough for thee, dost thou desire more?
Alas! the Gods will give nought else from their eternal store.

For our high Gods have sick and wearied grown
  Of all our endless sins, our vain endeavour
For wasted days of youth to make atone
  By pain or prayer or priest, and never, never,
Hearken they now to either good or ill,
But send their rain upon the just and the unjust at will.

They sit at ease, our Gods they sit at ease,
   Strewing with leaves of rose their scented wine,
They sleep, they sleep, beneath the rocking trees
   Where asphodel and yellow lotus twine,
Mourning the old glad days before they knew
What evil things the heart of man could dream, and dreaming do.

 And far beneath the brazen floor they see
   Like swarming flies the crowd of little men,
The bustle of small lives, then wearily
   Back to their lotus-haunts they turn again
Kissing each other's mouths, and mix more deep T
he poppy-seeded draught which brings soft purple-lidded sleep.

 There all day long the golden-vestured sun,
   Their torch-bearer, stands with his torch a-blaze,
And when the gaudy web of noon is spun
   By its twelve maidens through the crimson haze
Fresh from Endymion's arms comes forth the moon,
And the immortal Gods in toils of mortal passions swoon.

 There walks Queen Juno through some dewy mead
   Her grand white feet flecked with the saffron dust
Of wind-stirred lilies, while young Ganymede
   Leaps in the hot and amber-foaming must,
His curls all tossed, as when the eagle bare
The frightened boy from Ida through the blue Ionian air.

 There in the green heart of some garden close
   Queen Venus with the shepherd at her side,
Her warm soft body like the briar rose
   Which would be white yet blushes at its pride,
Laughs low for love, till jealous Salmacis
Peers through the myrtle-leaves and sighs for pain of lonely bliss.

There never does that dreary north-wind blow
  Which leaves our English forests bleak and bare,
Nor ever falls the swift white-feathered snow,
  Nor doth the red-toothed lightning ever dare
To wake them in the silver-fretted night
When we lie weeping for some sweet sad sin, some dead delight.

Alas! they know the far Lethæan spring,
  The violet-hidden waters well they know,
Where one whose feet with tired wandering
  Are faint and broken may take heart and go,
And from those dark depths cool and crystalline
Drink, and draw balm, and sleep for sleepless souls, and anodyne.

But we oppress our natures, God or Fate
  Is our enemy, we starve and feed
On vain repentance—O we are born too late!
  What balm for us in bruisèd poppy seed
Who crowd into one finite pulse of time
The joy of infinite love and the fierce pain of infinite crime.

O we are wearied of this sense of guilt,
  Wearied of pleasure's paramour despair,
Wearied of every temple we have built,
  Wearied of every right, unanswered prayer,
For man is weak; God sleeps: and heaven is high:
One fiery-coloured moment: one great love; and lo! we die.

Ah! but no ferry-man with labouring pole
  Nears his black shallop to the flowerless strand,
No little coin of bronze can bring the soul
  Over Death's river to the sunless land,
Victim and wine and vow are all in vain,
The tomb is sealed; the soldiers watch; the dead rise not again.

We are resolved into the supreme air,
  We are made one with what we touch and see,
With our heart's blood each crimson sun is fair,
  With our young lives each spring-impassioned tree
Flames into green, the wildest beasts that range
The moor our kinsmen are, all life is one, and all is change.

With beat of systole and of diastole
  One grand great life throbs through earth's giant heart,
And mighty waves of single Being roll
  From nerve-less germ to man, for we are part
Of every rock and bird and beast and hill,
One with the things that prey on us, and one with what we kill.

From lower cells of waking life we pass
  To full perfection; thus the world grows old:
We who are godlike now were once a mass
  Of quivering purple flecked with bars of gold,
Unsentient or of joy or misery,
And tossed in terrible tangles of some wild and wind-swept sea.

This hot hard flame with which our bodies burn
  Will make some meadow blaze with daffodil,
Ay! and those argent breasts of thine will turn
  To water-lilies; the brown fields men till
Will be more fruitful for our love to-night,
Nothing is lost in nature, all things live in Death's despite.

The boy's first kiss, the hyacinth's first bell,
  The man's last passion, and the last red spear
That from the lily leaps, the asphodel
  Which will not let its blossoms blow for fear
Of too much beauty, and the timid shame
Of the young bride-groom at his lover's eyes,—these with the same

One sacrament are consecrate, the earth
  Not we alone hath passions hymeneal,
The yellow buttercups that shake for mirth
  At daybreak know a pleasure not less real
Than we do, when in some fresh-blossoming wood
  We draw the spring into our hearts, and feel that life is good.

So when men bury us beneath the yew
  Thy crimson-stainèd mouth a rose will be,
And thy soft eyes lush bluebells dimmed with dew,
  And when the white narcissus wantonly
Kisses the wind its playmate, some faint joy
Will thrill our dust, and we will be again fond maid and boy.

And thus without life's conscious torturing pain
   In some sweet flower we will feel the sun,
And from the linnet's throat will sing again,
   And as two gorgeous-mailèd snakes will run
Over our graves, or as two tigers creep
Through the hot jungle where the yellow-eyed huge lions sleep

And give them battle! How my heart leaps up
   To think of that grand living after death
In beast and bird and flower, when this cup,
   Being filled too full of spirit, bursts for breath,
And with the pale leaves of some autumn day
The soul earth's earliest conqueror becomes earth's last great prey.

O think of it! We shall inform ourselves
   Into all sensuous life, the goat-foot Faun,
The Centaur, or the merry bright-eyed Elves
   That leave their dancing rings to spite the dawn
Upon the meadows, shall not be more near
Than you and I to nature's mysteries, for we shall hear

The thrush's heart beat, and the daisies grow,
   And the wan snowdrop sighing for the sun
On sunless days in winter, we shall know
   By whom the silver gossamer is spun,
Who paints the diapered fritillaries,
On what wide wings from shivering pine to pine the eagle flies.

Ay! had we never loved at all, who knows
   If yonder daffodil had lured the bee
Into its gilded womb, or any rose
   Had hung with crimson lamps its little tree!
Methinks no leaf would ever bud in spring,
But for the lovers' lips that kiss, the poets' lips that sing.

Is the light vanished from our golden sun,
   Or is this dædal-fashioned earth less fair,
That we are nature's heritors, and one
   With every pulse of life that beats the air?
Rather new suns across the sky shall pass,
New splendour come unto the flower, new glory to the grass.

And we two lovers shall not sit afar,
   Critics of nature, but the joyous sea
Shall be our raiment, and the bearded star
   Shoot arrows at our pleasure! We shall be
Part of the mighty universal whole,
And through all æons mix and mingle with the Kosmic Soul!

 We shall be notes in that great Symphony
   Whose cadence circles through the rhythmic spheres,
And all the live World's throbbing heart shall be
   One with our heart, the stealthy creeping years
Have lost their terrors now, we shall not die,
The Universe itself shall be our Immortality!

DOROTHY PARKER

"I like to have a martini,
Two at the very most.
After three I'm under the table,
after four I'm under my host."

MEN: A HATE SONG

I hate men.
They irritate me.

I

There are the Serious Thinkers,—
There ought to be a law against them.
They see life, as through shell-rimmed glasses, darkly.
They are always drawing their weary hands
Across their wan brows.
They talk about Humanity
As if they had just invented it;
They have to keep helping it along.
They revel in strikes
And they are eternally getting up petitions.
They are doing a wonderful thing for the Great Unwashed,—
They are living right down among them.
They can hardly wait
For "The Masses" to appear on the newsstands,
And they read all those Russian novels,—
The sex best sellers.

II

There are the Cave Men,—
The Specimens of Red-Blooded Manhood.
They eat everything very rare,
They are scarcely ever out of their cold baths,
And they want everybody to feel their muscles.
They talk in loud voices,
Using short Anglo-Saxon words.
They go around raising windows,
And they slap people on the back,
And tell them what they need is exercise.
They are always just on the point of walking to San Francisco,

Or crossing the ocean in a sailboat,
Or going through Russia on a sled—
I wish to God they would!

III

And then there are the Sensitive Souls
Who do interior decorating, for Art's sake.
They always smell faintly of vanilla
And put drops of sandalwood on their cigarettes.
They are continually getting up costume balls
So that they can go
As something out of the "Arabian Nights."
They give studio teas
Where people sit around on cushions
And wish they hadn't come.
They look at a woman languorously, through half-closed eyes,
And tell her, in low, passionate tones,
What she ought to wear.
Color is everything to them,—everything;
The wrong shade of purple
Gives them a nervous breakdown.

IV

Then there are the ones
Who are Simply Steeped in Crime.
They tell you how they haven't been to bed
For four nights.
They frequent those dramas
Where the only good lines
Are those of the chorus.
They stagger from one cabaret to another,
And they give you the exact figures of their gambling debts.
They hint darkly at the terrible part
That alcohol plays in their lives.
And then they shake their heads
And say Heaven must decide what is going to become of them,—
I wish I were Heaven!

I hate men.
They irritate me.

SUCH A PRETTY LITTLE PICTURE

I

Mr. Wheelock was clipping the hedge. He did not dislike doing it. If it had not been for the faintly sickish odor of the privet bloom, he would definitely have enjoyed it. The new shears were so sharp and bright, there was such a gratifying sense of something done as the young green stems snapped off and the expanse of tidy, square hedge-top lengthened. There was a lot of work to be done on it. It should have been attended to a week ago, but this was the first day that Mr. Wheelock had been able to get back from the city before dinnertime.

Clipping the hedge was one of the few domestic duties that Mr. Wheelock could be trusted with. He was notoriously poor at doing anything around the house. All the suburb knew about it. It was the source of all Mrs. Wheelock's jokes. Her most popular anecdote was of how, the past winter, he had gone out and hired a man to take care of the furnace, after a seven-years' losing struggle with it. She had an admirable memory, and often as she had related the story, she never dropped a word of it. Even now, in the late summer, she could hardly tell it for laughing.

When they were first married, Mr. Wheelock had lent himself to the fun. He had even posed as being more inefficient than he really was, to make the joke better. But he had tired of his helplessness, as a topic of conversation. All the men of Mrs. Wheelock's acquaintance, her cousins, her brother-in-law, the boys she went to high school with, the neighbors' husbands, were adepts at putting up a shelf, at repairing a lock, or making a shirtwaist box. Mr. Wheelock had begun to feel that there was something rather effeminate about his lack of interest in such things.

He had wanted to answer his wife, lately, when she enlivened some neighbor's dinner table with tales of his inadequacy with hammer and wrench. He had wanted to cry, "All right, suppose I'm not any good at things like that. What of it?"

He had played with the idea, had tried to imagine how his voice would sound, uttering the words. But he could think of no further argument for his case than that "What of it?" And he was a little relieved, somehow, at being able to find nothing stronger. It made it reassuringly impossible to go through with the plan of answering his wife's public railleries.

Mrs. Wheelock sat, now, on the spotless porch of the neat stucco house. Beside her was a pile of her husband's shirts and drawers, the price-tags still on them. She was going over all the buttons before he wore the garments, sewing them on more firmly. Mrs. Wheelock never waited for a button to come off, before sewing it on. She worked with quick, decided movements, compressing her lips each time the thread made a slight resistance to her deft jerks.

She was not a tall woman, and since the birth of her child she had gone over from a delicate plumpness to a settled stockiness. Her brown hair, though abundant, grew in an uncertain line about her forehead. It was her habit to put it up in curlers at night, but the crimps never came out in the right place. It was arranged with perfect neatness, yet it suggested that it had been done up and got over with as quickly as possible. Passionately clean, she was always redolent of the germicidal soap she used so vigorously. She was wont to tell people, somewhat redundantly, that she never employed any sort of cosmetics. She had unlimited contempt for women who sought to reduce their weight by dieting, cutting from their menus such nourishing items as cream and puddings and cereals.

Adelaide Wheelock's friends—and she had many of them—said of her that there was no nonsense about her. They and she regarded it as a compliment.

Sister, the Wheelocks' five-year-old daughter, played quietly in the gravel path that divided the tiny lawn. She had been known as Sister since her birth, and her mother still laid plans for a brother for her. Sister's baby carriage stood waiting in the cellar, her baby clothes were stacked expectantly away in bureau drawers. But raises were infrequent at the advertising agency where Mr. Wheelock was employed, and his present salary had barely caught up to the cost of their living. They could not conscientiously regard themselves as being able to afford a son. Both Mr. and Mrs. Wheelock keenly felt his guilt in keeping the bassinet empty.

Sister was not a pretty child, though her features were straight, and her eyes would one day be handsome. The left one turned slightly in toward the nose, now, when she looked in a certain direction; they would operate as soon as she was seven. Her hair was pale and limp, and her color bad. She was a delicate little girl. Not fragile in a picturesque way, but the kind of child that must be always undergoing treatment for its teeth and its throat and obscure things in its nose. She had lately had her adenoids removed, and she was still using squares of surgical gauze in stead of handkerchiefs. Both she and her mother somehow felt that these gave her a sort of prestige.

She was additionally handicapped by her frocks, which her mother bought a size or so too large, with a view to Sister's growing into them—an expectation which seemed never to be realized, for her skirts were always too long, and the shoulders of her little dresses came halfway down to her thin elbows. Yet, even discounting the unfortunate way she was dressed, you could tell, in some way, that she was never going to wear any kind of clothes well.

Mr. Wheelock glanced at her now and then as he clipped. He had never felt any fierce thrills of father-love for the child. He had been disappointed in her when she was a pale, large-headed baby, smelling of stale milk and warm rubber. Sister made him feel ill at ease, vaguely irritated him. He had had no share in her training; Mrs. Wheelock was so competent a parent that she took the places of both of them. When Sister came to him to ask his permission to do something, he always told her to wait and ask her mother about it.

He regarded himself as having the usual paternal affection for his daughter. There were times, indeed, when she had tugged sharply at his heart—when he had waited in the corridor outside the operating room; when she was still under the anesthetic, and lay little and white and helpless on her high hospital bed; once when he had accidentally closed a door upon her thumb. But from the first he had nearly acknowledged to himself that he did not like Sister as a person.

Sister was not a whining child, despite her poor health. She had always been sensible and well-mannered, amenable about talking to visitors, rigorously unselfish. She never got into trouble, like other children. She did not care much for other children. She had heard herself described as being "old-fashioned," and she knew she was delicate, and she felt that these attributes rather set her above them. Besides, they were rough and careless of their bodily well-being.

Sister was exquisitely cautious of her safety. Grass, she knew, was often apt to be damp in the late afternoon, so she was careful now to stay right in the middle of the gravel path, sitting on a folded newspaper and playing one of her mysterious games with three petunias that she had been allowed to pick. Mrs. Wheelock never had to speak to her twice about keeping off wet grass, or wearing her rubbers, or putting on her jacket if a breeze sprang up. Sister was an immediately obedient child, always.

II

Mrs. Wheelock looked up from her sewing and spoke to her husband. Her voice was high and clear, resolutely good-humored. From her habit of calling instructions from her upstairs window to Sister playing on the porch below, she spoke always a little louder than was necessary.

"Daddy," she said.

She had called him Daddy since some eight months before Sister was born. She and the child had the same trick of calling his name and then waiting until he signified that he was attending before they went on with what they wanted to say.

Mr. Wheelock stopped clipping, straightened himself and turned toward her.

"Daddy," she went on, thus reassured, "I saw Mr. Ince down at the post office today when Sister and I went down to get the ten o'clock mail—there wasn't much, just a card for me from Grace Williams from that place they go to up on Cape Cod, and an advertisement from some department store or other about their summer fur sale (as if I cared!), and a circular for you from the bank. I opened it; I knew you wouldn't mind.

"Anyway, I just thought I'd tackle Mr. Ince first as last about getting in our cordwood. He didn't see me at first—though I'll bet he really saw me and pretended not to—but I ran right after him. 'Oh, Mr. Ince!' I said. 'Why, hello, Mrs. Wheelock,' he said, and then he asked for you, and I told him you were finely, and everything. Then I said, 'Now, Mr. Ince,' I said, 'how about getting in that cordwood of ours?' And he said, 'Well, Mrs. Wheelock,' he said, 'I'll get it in soon's I can, but I'm short of help right now,' he said.

"Short of help! Of course I couldn't say anything, but I guess he could tell from the way I looked at him how much I believed it. I just said, 'All right, Mr. Ince, but don't you forget us. There may be a cold snap coming on,' I said, 'and we'll be wanting a fire in the living-room. Don't you forget us,' I said, and he said, no, he wouldn't.

"If that wood isn't here by Monday, I think you ought to do something about it, Daddy. There's no sense in all this putting it off, and putting it off. First thing you know there'll be a cold snap coming on, and we'll be wanting a fire in the living-room, and there we'll be! You'll be sure and 'tend to it, won't you, Daddy? I'll remind you again Monday, if I can think of it, but there are so many things!"

Mr. Wheelock nodded and turned back to his clipping—and his thoughts. They were thoughts that had occupied much of his leisure lately. After dinner, when Adelaide was sewing or arguing with the maid, he found himself letting his magazine fall face downward on his knee, while he rolled the same idea round and round in his mind. He had got so that he looked forward, through the day, to losing himself in it. He had rather welcomed the hedge-clipping; you can clip and think at the same time.

It had started with a story that he had picked up somewhere. He couldn't recall whether he had heard it or had read it—that was probably it, he thought, he had run across it in the back pages of some comic paper that someone had left on the train.

It was about a man who lived in a suburb. Every morning he had gone to the city on the 8:12, sitting in the same seat in the same car, and every evening he had gone home to his wife on the 5:17, sitting in the same seat in the same car. He had done this for twenty years of his life. And then one night he didn't come home. He never went back to his office any more. He just never turned up again.

The last man to see him was the conductor on the 5:17.

"He came down the platform at the Grand Central," the man reported, "just like he done every night since I been working on this road. He put one foot on the step, and then he stopped sudden, and he said 'Oh, hell,' and he took his foot off of the step and walked away. And that's the last anybody see of him."

Curious how that story took hold of Mr. Wheelock's fancy. He had started thinking of it as a mildly humorous anecdote; he had come to accept it as fact. He did not think the man's sitting in the same seat in the same car need have been stressed so much. That seemed unimportant. He thought long about the man's wife, wondered what suburb he had lived in. He loved to play with the thing, to try to feel what the man felt before he took his foot off the car's step. He never concerned himself with speculations as to where the man had disappeared, how he had spent the rest of his life. Mr. Wheelock was absorbed in that moment when he had said "Oh, hell," and walked off. "Oh, hell" seemed to Mr. Wheelock a fine thing for him to have said, a perfect summary of the situation.

He tried thinking of himself in the man's place. But no, he would have done it from the other end. That was the real way to do it.

Some summer evening like this, say, when Adelaide was sewing on buttons, up on the porch, and Sister was playing somewhere about. A pleasant, quiet evening it must be, with the shadows lying long on the street that led from their house to the station. He would put down the garden shears, or the hose, or whatever he happened to be puttering with—not throw the thing down, you know, just put it quietly aside—and walk out of the gate and down the street, and that would be the last they'd see of him. He would time it so that he'd just make the 6:03 for the city comfortably.

He did not go ahead with it from there, much. He was not especially anxious to leave the advertising agency forever. He did not particularly dislike his work. He had been an advertising solicitor since he had gone to work at all, and he worked hard at his job and, aside from that, didn't think about it much one way or the other.

It seemed to Mr. Wheelock that before he had got hold of the "Oh, hell" story he had never thought about anything much, one way or the other. But he would have to disappear from the office, too, that was certain. It would spoil everything to turn up there again. He thought dimly of taking a train going West, after the 6:03 got him to the Grand Central Terminal—he might go to Buffalo, say, or perhaps Chicago. Better just let that part take care of itself and go back to dwell on the moment when it would sweep over him that he was going to do it, when he would put down the shears and walk out the gate—

The "Oh, hell" rather troubled him. Mr. Wheelock felt that he would like to retain that; it completed the gesture so beautifully. But he didn't quite know to whom he should say it.

He might stop in at the post office on his way to the station and say it to the postmaster; but the postmaster would probably think he was only annoyed at there being no mail for him. Nor would the conductor of the 6:03, a train Mr. Wheelock never used, take the right interest in it. Of course the real thing to do would be to say it to Adelaide just before he laid down the shears. But somehow Mr. Wheelock could not make that scene come very clear in his imagination.

III

"Daddy," Mrs. Wheelock said briskly.

He stopped clipping, and faced her.

"Daddy," she related, "I saw Doctor Mann's automobile going by the house this morning—he was going to have a look at Mr. Warren, his rheumatism's getting along nicely—and I called him in a minute, to look us over."

She screwed up her face, winked, and nodded vehemently several times in the direction of the absorbed Sister, to indicate that she was the subject of the discourse.

"He said we were going ahead finely," she resumed, when she was sure that he had caught the idea. "Said there was no need for those t-o-n-s-i-l-s to c-o-m-e o-u-t. But I thought, soon's it gets a little cooler, some time next month, we'd just run in to the city and let Doctor Sturges have a look at us. I'd rather be on the safe side."

"But Doctor Lytton said it wasn't necessary, and those doctors at the hospital, and now Doctor Mann, that's known her since she was a baby," suggested Mr. Wheelock.

"I know, I know," replied his wife. "But I'd rather be on the safe side."

Mr. Wheelock went back to his hedge.

Oh, of course he couldn't do it; he never seriously thought he could, for a minute. Of course he couldn't. He wouldn't have the shadow of an excuse for doing it. Adelaide was a sterling woman, an utterly faithful wife, an almost slavish mother. She ran his house economically and efficiently. She harried the suburban trades people into giving them dependable service, drilled the succession of poorly paid, poorly trained maids, cheerfully did the thousand fussy little things that go with the running of a house. She looked after his clothes, gave him medicine when she thought he needed it, oversaw the preparation of every meal that was set before him; they were not especially inspirational meals, but the food was always nourishing and, as a general thing, fairly well cooked. She never lost her temper, she was never depressed, never ill.

Not the shadow of an excuse. People would know that, and so they would invent an excuse for him. They would say there must be another woman.

Mr. Wheelock frowned, and snipped at an obstinate young twig. Good Lord, the last thing he wanted was another woman. What he wanted was that moment when he realized he could do it, when he would lay down the shears—

Oh, of course he couldn't; he knew that as well as anybody. What would they do, Adelaide and Sister? The house wasn't even paid for yet, and there would be that operation on Sister's eye in a couple of years. But the house would be all paid up by next March. And there was always that well-to-do brother-in- law of Adelaide's, the one who, for all his means, put up every shelf in that great big house with his own hands.

Decent people didn't just go away and leave their wives and families that way. All right, suppose you weren't decent; what of it? Here was Adelaide planning what she was going to do when it got a little cooler, next month. She was always planning ahead, always confident that things would go on just the same. Naturally, Mr. Wheelock realized that he couldn't do it, as well as the next one. But there was no harm in fooling around with the idea. Would you say the "Oh, hell" now, before you laid down the shears, or right after? How would it be to turn at the gate and say it?

Mr. and Mrs. Fred Coles came down the street arm-in-arm, from their neat stucco house on the corner.

"See they've got you working hard, eh?" cried Mr. Coles genially, as they paused abreast of the hedge.

Mr. Wheelock laughed politely, marking time for an answer.

"That's right," he evolved.

Mrs. Wheelock looked up from her work, shading her eyes with her thimbled hand against the long rays of the low sun.

"Yes, we finally got Daddy to do a little work," she called brightly. "But Sister and I are staying right here to watch over him, for fear he might cut his little self with the shears."

There was general laughter, in which Sister joined. She had risen punctiliously at the approach of the older people, and she was looking politely at their eyes, as she had been taught.

"And how is my great big girl?" asked Mrs. Coles, gazing fondly at the child.

"Oh, much better," Mrs. Wheelock answered for her. "Doctor Mann says we are going ahead finely. I saw his automobile passing the house this morning—he was going to see Mr. Warren, his rheumatism's coming along nicely—and I called him in a minute to look us over."

She did the wink and the nods, at Sister's back. Mr. and Mrs. Coles nodded shrewdly back at her.

"He said there's no need for those t-o-n-s-i-l-s to c-o-m-e o-u-t," Mrs. Wheelock called. "But I thought, soon's it gets a little cooler, some time next month, we'd just run in to the city and let Doctor Sturges have a look at us. I was telling Daddy, 'I'd rather be on the safe side,' I said."

"Yes, it's better to be on the safe side," agreed Mrs. Coles, and her husband nodded again, sagely this time. She took his arm, and they moved slowly off.

"Been a lovely day, hasn't it?" she said over her shoulder, fearful of having left too abruptly. "Fred and I are taking a little constitutional before supper."

"Oh, taking a little constitutional?" cried Mrs. Wheelock, laughing.

Mrs. Coles laughed also, three or four bars.

"Yes, just taking a little constitutional before supper," she called back.

Sister, weary of her game, mounted the porch, whimpering a little. Mrs. Wheelock put aside her sewing, and took the tired child in her lap. The sun's last rays touched her brown hair, making it a shimmering gold. Her small, sharp face, the thick lines of her figure were in shadow as she bent over the little girl. Sister's head was hidden on her mother's shoulder, the folds of her rumpled white frock followed her limp, relaxed little body.

The lovely light was kind to the cheap, hurriedly built stucco house, to the clean gravel path, and the bits of closely cut lawn. It was gracious, too, to Mr. Wheelock's tall, lean figure as he bent to work on the last few inches of unclipped hedge.

Twenty years, he thought. The man in the story went through with it for twenty years. He must have been a man along around forty-five, most likely. Mr. Wheelock was thirty-seven. Eight years. It's a long time, eight years is. You could easily get so you could say that final "Oh, hell," even to Adelaide, in eight years. It probably wouldn't take more than four for you to know that you could do it. No, not more than two....

Mrs. Coles paused at the corner of the Street and looked back at the Wheelocks' house. The last of the light lingered on the mother and child group on the porch, gently touched the tall, white-clad figure of the husband and father as he went up to them, his work done.

Mrs. Coles was a large, soft woman, barren, and addicted to sentiment.

"Look, Fred; just turn around and look at that," she said to her husband. She looked again, sighing luxuriously. "Such a pretty little picture!"

REFORMERS: A HYMN OF HATE

I hate Reformers;
They raise my blood pressure.

There are the Prohibitionists;
The Fathers of Bootlegging.
They made us what we are to-day—
I hope they're satisfied.
They can prove that the Johnstown flood,
And the blizzard of 1888,
And the destruction of Pompeii
Were all due to alcohol.
They have it figured out
That anyone who would give a gin daisy a friendly look
Is just wasting time out of jail,
And anyone who would stay under the same roof
With a bottle of Scotch
Is right in line for a cozy seat in the electric chair.
They fixed things all up pretty for us;
Now that they have dried up the country,
You can hardly get a drink unless you go in and order one.
They are in a nasty state over this light wines and beer idea;
They say that lips that touch liquor
Shall never touch wine.
They swear that the Eighteenth Amendment
Shall be improved upon

Over their dead bodies—
Fair enough!
Then there are the Suppressors of Vice;
The Boys Who Made the Name of Cabell a Household Word.
Their aim is to keep art and letters in their place;
If they see a book
Which does not come right out and say
That the doctor brings babies in his little black bag,

Or find a painting of a young lady
Showing her without her rubbers,
They call out the militia.
They have a mean eye for dirt;
They can find it
In a copy of "What Katy Did at School,"
Or a snapshot of Aunt Bessie in bathing at Sandy Creek,
Or a picture postcard of Moonlight in Bryant Park.
They are always running around suppressing things,
Beginning with their desires.
They get a lot of excitement out of life,—
They are constantly discovering
The New Rabelais
Or the Twentieth Century Hogarth.
Their leader is regarded
As the representative of Comstock here on earth.
How does that song of Tosti's go?—
"Good-bye, Sumner, good-bye, good-bye."

There are the Movie Censors,
The motion picture is still in its infancy,—
They are the boys who keep it there.
If the film shows a party of clubmen tossing off ginger ale,
Or a young bride dreaming over tiny garments,
Or Douglas Fairbanks kissing Mary Pickford's hand,
They cut out the scene
And burn it in the public square.
They fix up all the historical events
So that their own mothers wouldn't know them.
They make Du Barry Mrs. Louis Fifteenth,
And show that Anthony and Cleopatra were like brother and sister,
And announce Salome's engagement to John the Baptist,
So that the audiences won't go and get ideas in their heads.
They insist that Sherlock Holmes is made to say,
"Quick, Watson, the crochet needle!"
And the state pays them for it.
They say they are going to take the sin out of cinema
If they perish in the attempt,—
I wish to God they would!
And then there are the All-American Crabs;
The Brave Little Band that is Against Everything.

They have got up the idea
That things are not what they were when Grandma was a girl.
They say that they don't know what we're coming to,
As if they had just written the line.
They are always running a temperature
Over the modern dances,
Or the new skirts,
Or the goings-on of the younger set.
They can barely hold themselves in
When they think of the menace of the drama;
They seem to be going ahead under the idea
That everything but the Passion Play
Was written by Avery Hopwood.
They will never feel really themselves
Until every theatre in the country is razed.
They are forever signing petitions
Urging that cigarette-smokers should be deported,
And that all places of amusement should be closed on Sunday
And kept closed all week.
They take everything personally;
They go about shaking their heads,
And sighing, "It's all wrong, it's all wrong,"—
They said it.

I hate Reformers;
They raise my blood pressure.

F. SCOTT FITZGERALD

*"Here's to alcohol,
the rose colored glasses of life."*

THE BEAUTIFUL AND DAMNED (EXCERPT)

THE CATASTROPHE

Early September in Camp Boone, Mississippi. The darkness, alive with insects, beat in upon the mosquito-netting, beneath the shelter of which Anthony was trying to write a letter. An intermittent chatter over a poker game was going on in the next tent, and outside a man was strolling up the company street singing a current bit of doggerel about "K-K-K-Katy."

With an effort Anthony hoisted himself to his elbow and, pencil in hand, looked down at his blank sheet of paper. Then, omitting any heading, he began:

I can't imagine what the matter is, Gloria. I haven't had a line from you for two weeks and it's only natural to be worried—

He threw this away with a disturbed grunt and began again:

I don't know what to think, Gloria. Your last letter, short, cold, without a word of affection or even a decent account of what you've been doing, came two weeks ago. It's only natural that I should wonder. If your love for me isn't absolutely dead it seems that you'd at least keep me from worry—

Again he crumpled the page and tossed it angrily through a tear in the tent wall, realizing simultaneously that he would have to pick it up in the morning. He felt disinclined to try again. He could get no warmth into the lines—only a persistent jealousy and suspicion. Since midsummer these discrepancies in Gloria's correspondence had grown more and more noticeable. At first he had scarcely perceived them. He was so inured to the perfunctory "dearest" and "darlings" scattered through her letters that he was oblivious to their presence or absence. But in this last fortnight he had become increasingly aware that there was something amiss.

He had sent her a night-letter saying that he had passed his examinations for an officers' training-camp, and expected to leave for Georgia shortly. She had not answered. He had wired again—when he received no word he imagined that she might be out of town. But it occurred and recurred to him that she was not out of town, and a series of distraught imaginings began to plague him. Supposing Gloria, bored and restless, had found someone, even as he had. The thought terrified him with its possibility—it was chiefly because he had been so sure of her personal integrity that he had considered her so sparingly during the year. And now, as a doubt was born, the old angers, the rages of possession, swarmed back a thousandfold. What more natural than that she should be in love again?

He remembered the Gloria who promised that should she ever want anything, she would take it, insisting that since she would act entirely for her own satisfaction she could go through such an affair unsmirched—it was only the effect on a person's mind that counted, anyhow, she said, and her reaction would be the masculine one, of satiation and faint dislike.

But that had been when they were first married. Later, with the discovery that she could be jealous of Anthony, she had, outwardly at least, changed her mind. There were no other men in the world for her. This he had known only too surely. Perceiving that a certain fastidiousness would restrain her, he had grown lax in preserving the completeness of her love—which, after all, was the keystone of the entire structure.

Meanwhile all through the summer he had been maintaining Dot in a boarding-house down-town. To do this it had been necessary to write to his broker for money. Dot had covered her journey south by leaving her house a day before the brigade broke camp, informing her mother in a note that she had gone to New York. On the evening following Anthony had called as though to see her. Mrs. Raycroft was in a state of collapse and there was a policeman in the parlor. A questionnaire had ensued, from which Anthony had extricated himself with some difficulty.

In September, with his suspicions of Gloria, the company of Dot had become tedious, then almost intolerable. He was nervous and irritable from lack of sleep; his heart was sick and afraid. Three days ago he had gone to Captain Dunning and asked for a furlough, only to be met with benignant procrastination. The division was starting overseas, while Anthony was going to an officers' training-camp; what furloughs could be given must go to the men who were leaving the country.

Upon this refusal Anthony had started to the telegraph office intending to wire Gloria to come South—he reached the door and receded despairingly, seeing the utter impracticability of such a move. Then he had spent the evening quarrelling irritably with Dot, and returned to camp morose and angry with the world. There had been a disagreeable scene, in the midst of which he had precipitately departed. What was to be done with her did not seem to concern him vitally at present—he was completely absorbed in the disheartening silence of his wife....

The flap of the tent made a sudden triangle back upon itself, and a dark head appeared against the night.

"Sergeant Patch?" The accent was Italian, and Anthony saw by the belt that the man was a headquarters orderly.

"Want me?"

"Lady call up headquarters ten minutes ago. Say she have speak with you. Ver' important."

Anthony swept aside the mosquito-netting and stood up. It might be a wire from Gloria telephoned over.

"She say to get you. She call again ten o'clock."

"All right, thanks." He picked up his hat and in a moment was striding beside the orderly through the hot, almost suffocating, darkness. Over in the headquarters shack he saluted a dozing night-service officer.

"Sit down and wait," suggested the lieutenant nonchalantly. "Girl seemed awful anxious to speak to you."

Anthony's hopes fell away.

"Thank you very much, sir." And as the phone squeaked on the side-wall he knew who was calling.

"This is Dot," came an unsteady voice, "I've got to see you."

"Dot, I told you I couldn't get down for several days."

"I've got to see you to-night. It's important."

"It's too late," he said coldly; "it's ten o'clock, and I have to be in camp at eleven."

"All right." There was so much wretchedness compressed into the two words that Anthony felt a measure of compunction.

"What's the matter?"

"I want to tell you good-by."

"Oh, don't be a little idiot!" he exclaimed. But his spirits rose. What luck if she should leave town this very night! What a burden from his soul. But he said: "You can't possibly leave before to-morrow."

Out of the corner of his eye he saw the night-service officer regarding him quizzically. Then, startlingly, came Dot's next words:

"I don't mean 'leave' that way."

Anthony's hand clutched the receiver fiercely. He felt his nerves turning cold as if the heat was leaving his body.

"What?"

Then quickly in a wild broken voice he heard·

"Good-by—oh, good-by!"

Cul-lup! She had hung up the receiver. With a sound that was half a gasp, half a cry, Anthony hurried from the headquarters building. Outside, under the stars that dripped like silver tassels through the trees of the little grove, he stood motionless, hesitating. Had she meant to kill herself?—oh, the little fool! He was filled with bitter hate toward her. In this dénouement he found it impossible to realize that he had ever begun such an entanglement, such a mess, a sordid mélange of worry and pain.

He found himself walking slowly away, repeating over and over that it was futile to worry. He had best go back to his tent and sleep. He needed sleep. God! Would he ever sleep again? His mind was in a vast clamor and confusion; as he reached the road he turned around in a panic and began running, not toward his company but away from it. Men were returning now—he could find a taxicab. After a minute two yellow eyes appeared around a bend. Desperately he ran toward them.

"Jitney! Jitney!" ... It was an empty Ford.... "I want to go to town."

"Cost you a dollar."

"All right. If you'll just hurry—"

After an interminable time he ran up the steps of a dark ramshackle little house, and through the door, almost knocking over an immense negress who was walking, candle in hand, along the hall.

"Where's my wife?" he cried wildly.

"She gone to bed."

Up the stairs three at a time, down the creaking passage. The room was dark and silent, and with trembling fingers he struck a match. Two wide eyes looked up at him from a wretched ball of clothes on the bed.

"Ah, I knew you'd come," she murmured brokenly.

Anthony grew cold with anger.

"So it was just a plan to get me down here, get me in trouble!" he said. "God damn it, you've shouted 'wolf' once too often!"

She regarded him pitifully.

"I had to see you. I couldn't have lived. Oh, I had to see you—"

He sat down on the side of the bed and slowly shook his head.

"You're no good," he said decisively, talking unconsciously as Gloria might have talked to him. "This sort of thing isn't fair to me, you know."

"Come closer." Whatever he might say Dot was happy now. He cared for her. She had brought him to her side.

"Oh, God," said Anthony hopelessly. As weariness rolled along its inevitable wave his anger subsided, receded, vanished. He collapsed suddenly, fell sobbing beside her on the bed.

"Oh, my darling," she begged him, "don't cry! Oh, don't cry!"

She took his head upon her breast and soothed him, mingled her happy tears with the bitterness of his. Her hand played gently with his dark hair.

"I'm such a little fool," she murmured brokenly, "but I love you, and when you're cold to me it seems as if it isn't worth while to go on livin'."

After all, this was peace—the quiet room with the mingled scent of women's powder and perfume, Dot's hand soft as a warm wind upon his hair, the rise and fall of her bosom as she took breath—for a moment it was as though it were Gloria there, as though he were at rest in some sweeter and safer home than he had ever known.

An hour passed. A clock began to chime in the hall. He jumped to his feet and looked at the phosphorescent hands of his wrist watch. It was twelve o'clock.

He had trouble in finding a taxi that would take him out at that hour. As he urged the driver faster along the road he speculated on the best method of entering camp. He had been late several times recently, and he knew that were he caught again his name would probably be stricken from the list of officer candidates. He wondered if he had not better dismiss the taxi and take a chance on passing the sentry in the dark. Still, officers often rode past the sentries after midnight....

"Halt!" The monosyllable came from the yellow glare that the headlights dropped upon the changing road. The taxi-driver threw out his clutch and a sentry walked up, carrying his rifle at the port. With him, by an ill chance, was the officer of the guard.

"Out late, sergeant."

"Yes, sir. Got delayed."

"Too bad. Have to take your name."

As the officer waited, note-book and pencil in hand, something not fully intended crowded to Anthony's lips, something born of panic, of muddle, of despair.

"Sergeant R.A. Foley," he answered breathlessly.

"And the outfit?"

"Company Q, Eighty-third Infantry."

"All right. You'll have to walk from here, sergeant."

Anthony saluted, quickly paid his taxi-driver, and set off for a run toward the regiment he had named. When he was out of sight he changed his course, and with his heart beating wildly, hurried to his company, feeling that he had made a fatal error of judgment.

Two days later the officer who had been in command of the guard recognized him in a barber shop down-town. In charge of a military policeman he was taken back to the camp, where he was reduced to the ranks without trial, and confined for a month to the limits of his company street.

With this blow a spell of utter depression overtook him, and within a week he was again caught down-town, wandering around in a drunken daze, with a pint of bootleg whiskey in his hip pocket. It was because of a sort of craziness in his behavior at the trial that his sentence to the guard-house was for only three weeks.

JEMINA, THE MOUNTAIN GIRL

This don't pretend to be "Literature." This is just a tale for red-blooded folks who want a story and not just a lot of "psychological" stuff or "analysis." Boy, you'll love it! Read it here, see it in the movies, play it on the phonograph, run it through the sewing-machine.

A WILD THING

It was night in the mountains of Kentucky. Wild hills rose on all sides. Swift mountain streams flowed rapidly up and down the mountains.

Jemina Tantrum was down at the stream, brewing whiskey at the family still.

She was a typical mountain girl.

Her feet were bare. Her hands, large and powerful, hung down below her knees. Her face showed the ravages of work. Although but sixteen, she had for over a dozen years been supporting her aged pappy and mappy by brewing mountain whiskey. From time to time she would pause in her task, and, filling a dipper full of the pure, invigorating liquid, would drain it off—then pursue her work with renewed vigor.

She would place the rye in the vat, thresh it out with her feet and, in twenty minutes, the completed product would be turned out.

A sudden cry made her pause in the act of draining a dipper and look up.

"Hello," said a voice. It came from a man clad in hunting boots reaching to his neck, who had emerged.

"Can you tell me the way to the Tantrums' cabin?"

"Are you uns from the settlements down thar?"

She pointed her hand down to the bottom of the hill, where Louisville lay. She had never been there; but once, before she was born, her great-grandfather, old Gore Tantrum, had gone into the settlements in the company of two marshals, and had never come back. So the Tantrums from generation to generation, had learned to dread civilization.

The man was amused. He laughed a light tinkling laugh, the laugh of a Philadelphian. Something in the ring of it thrilled her. She drank off another dipper of whiskey.

"Where is Mr. Tantrum, little girl?" he asked, not without kindness.

She raised her foot and pointed her big toe toward the woods. "Thar in the cabing behind those thar pines. Old Tantrum air my old man."

The man from the settlements thanked her and strode off. He was fairly vibrant with youth and personality. As he walked along he whistled and sang and turned handsprings and flapjacks, breathing in the fresh, cool air of the mountains.

The air around the still was like wine.

Jemina Tantrum watched him entranced. No one like him had ever come into her life before.

She sat down on the grass and counted her toes. She counted eleven.

She had learned arithmetic in the mountain school.

A MOUNTAIN FEUD

Ten years before a lady from the settlements had opened a school on the mountain. Jemina had no money, but she had paid her way in whiskey, bringing a pailful to school every morning and leaving it on Miss Lafarge's desk. Miss Lafarge had died of delirium tremens after a year's teaching, and so Jemina's education had stopped.

Across the still stream, still another still was standing; It was that of the Doldrums. The Doldrums and the Tantrums never exchanged calls.

They hated each other.

Fifty years before old Jem Doldrum and old Jem Tantrum had quarrelled in the Tantrum cabin over a game of slapjack. Jem Doldrum had thrown the king of hearts in Jem Tantrum's face, and old Tantrum, enraged, had felled the old Doldrum with the nine of diamonds. Other Doldrums and Tantrums had joined in and the little cabin was soon filled with flying cards. Harstrum Doldrum, one of the younger Doldrums, lay stretched on the floor writing in agony, the ace of hearts crammed down his throat. Jem Tantrum, standing in the doorway; ran through suit after suit, his face alight with fiendish hatred. Old Mappy Tantrum stood on the table wetting down the Doldrums with hot whiskey. Old Heck Doldrum, having finally run out of trumps, was backed out of the cabin, striking left and right with his tobacco pouch, and gathering around him the rest of his clan. Then they mounted their steers and galloped furiously home.

That night old man Doldrum and his sons, vowing vengeance, had returned, put a ticktock on the Tantrum window, stuck a pin in the doorbell, and beaten a retreat.

A week later the Tantrums had put Cod Liver Oil in the Doldrums' still, and so, from year to year, the feud had continued, first one family being entirely wiped out, then the other.

THE BIRTH OF LOVE

Every day little Jemina worked the still on her side of the stream, and Boscoe Doldrum worked the still on his side.

Sometimes, with automatic inherited hatred, the feudists would throw whiskey at each other, and Jemina would come home smelling like a French table d'hôte.

But now Jemina was too thoughtful to look across the stream.

How wonderful the stranger had been and how oddly he was dressed! In her innocent way she had never believed that there were any civilized settlements at all, and she had put the belief in them down to the credulity of the mountain people.

She turned to go up to the cabin, and, as she turned something struck her in the neck. It was a sponge, thrown by Boscoe Doldrum—a sponge soaked in whiskey from his still on the other side of the stream.

"Hi, thar, Boscoe Doldrum," she shouted in her deep bass voice.

"Yo! Jemina Tantrum. Gosh ding yo'!" he returned.

She continued her way to the cabin.

The stranger was talking to her father. Gold had been discovered on the Tantrum land, and the stranger, Edgar Edison, was trying to buy the land for a song. He was considering what song to offer.

She sat upon her hands and watched him.

He was wonderful. When he talked his lips moved.

She sat upon the stove and watched him.

Suddenly there came a blood-curdling scream. The Tantrums rushed to the windows.

It was the Doldrums.

They had hitched their steers to trees and concealed themselves behind the bushes and flowers, and soon a perfect rattle of stones and bricks beat against the windows, bending them inward.

"Father! father!" shrieked Jemina.

Her father took down his slingshot from his slingshot rack on the wall and ran his hand lovingly over the elastic band. He stepped to a loophole. Old Mappy Tantrum stepped to the coalhole.

A MOUNTAIN BATTLE

The stranger was aroused at last. Furious to get at the Doldrums, he tried to escape from the house by crawling up the chimney. Then he thought there might be a door under the bead, but Jemina told him there was not. He hunted for doors under the beds and sofas, but each time Jemina pulled him out and told him there were no doors there. Furious with anger, he beat upon the door and hollered at the Doldrums. They did not answer him, but kept up their fusillade of bricks and stones against the window. Old Pappy Tantrum knew that just as soon as they were able to affect an aperture they would pour in and the fight would be over.

Then old Heck Doldrum, foaming at the mouth and expectorating on the ground, left and right, led the attack.

The terrific slingshots of Pappy Tantrum had not been without their effect. A master shot had disabled one Doldrum, and another Doldrum, shot almost incessantly through the abdomen, fought feebly on.

Nearer and nearer they approached the house.

"We must fly," shouted the stranger to Jemina. "I will sacrifice myself and bear you away."

"No," shouted Pappy Tantrum, his face begrimed. "You stay here and fit on. I will bar Jemina away. I will bar Mappy away. I will bar myself away."

The man from the settlements, pale and trembling with anger, turned to Ham Tantrum, who stood at the door throwing loophole after loophole at the advancing Doldrums.

"Will you cover the retreat?"

But Ham said that he too had Tantrums to bear away, but that he would leave himself here to help the stranger cover the retreat, if he could think of a way of doing it.

Soon smoke began to filter through the floor and ceiling. Shem Doldrum had come up and touched a match to old Japhet Tantrum's breath as he leaned from a loophole, and the alcoholic flames shot up on all sides.

The whiskey in the bathtub caught fire. The walls began to fall in.

Jemina and the man from the settlements looked at each other.

"Jemina," he whispered.

"Stranger," she answered,

"We will die together," he said. "If we had lived I would have taken you to the city and married you. With your ability to hold liquor, your social success would have been assured."

She caressed him idly for a moment, counting her toes softly to herself. The smoke grew thicker. Her left leg was on fire.

She was a human alcohol lamp.

Their lips met in one long kiss and then a wall fell on them and blotted them out.

"As One."

When the Doldrums burst through the ring of flame, they found them dead where they had fallen, their arms about each other.

Old Jem Doldrum was moved.

He took off his hat.

He filled it with whiskey and drank it off.

"They air dead," he said slowly, "they hankered after each other. The fit is over now. We must not part them."

So they threw them together into the stream and the two splashes they made were as one.

THE CUT-GLASS BOWL (EXCERPT)

Concerning Mrs. Harold Piper at thirty-five, opinion was divided—women said she was still handsome; men said she was pretty no longer. And this was probably because the qualities in her beauty that women had feared and men had followed had vanished. Her eyes were still as large and as dark and as sad, but the mystery had departed; their sadness was no longer eternal, only human, and she had developed a habit, when she was startled or annoyed, of twitching her brows together and blinking several times. Her mouth also had lost: the red had receded and the faint down-turning of its corners when she smiled, that had added to the sadness of the eyes and been vaguely mocking and beautiful, was quite gone. When she smiled now the corners of her lips turned up. Back in the days when she revelled in her own beauty Evylyn had enjoyed that smile of hers—she had accentuated it. When she stopped accentuating it, it faded out and the last of her mystery with it.

Evylyn had ceased accentuating her smile within a month after the Freddy Gedney affair. Externally things had gone an very much as they had before. But in those few minutes during which she had discovered how much she loved her husband, Evylyn had realized how indelibly she had hurt him. For a month she struggled against aching silences, wild reproaches and accusations—she pled with him, made quiet, pitiful little love to him, and he laughed at her bitterly—and then she, too, slipped gradually into silence and a shadowy, impenetrable barrier dropped between them. The surge of love that had risen in her she lavished on Donald, her little boy, realizing him almost wonderingly as a part of her life.

The next year a piling up of mutual interests and responsibilities and some stray flicker from the past brought husband and wife together again—but after a rather pathetic flood of passion Evylyn realized that her great opportunity was gone. There simply wasn't anything left. She might have been youth and love for both—but that time of silence had slowly dried up the springs of affection and her own desire to drink again of them was dead.

She began for the first time to seek women friends, to prefer books she had read before, to sew a little where she could watch her two children to whom she was devoted. She worried about little things—if she saw crumbs on the dinner-table her mind drifted off the conversation: she was receding gradually into middle age.

Her thirty-fifth birthday had been an exceptionally busy one, for they were entertaining on short notice that night, as she stood in her bedroom window in the late afternoon she discovered that she was quite tired. Ten years before she would have lain down and slept, but now she had a feeling that things needed watching: maids were cleaning down-stairs, bric-à-brac was all over the floor, and there were sure to be grocery-men that had to be talked to imperatively—and then there was a letter to write Donald, who was fourteen and in his first year away at school.

She had nearly decided to lie down, nevertheless, when she heard a sudden familiar signal from little Julie down-stairs. She compressed her lips, her brows twitched together, and she blinked.

"Julie!" she called.

"Ah-h-h-ow!" prolonged Julie plaintively. Then the voice of Hilda, the second maid, floated up the stairs.

"She cut herself a little, Mis' Piper."

Evylyn flew to her sewing-basket, rummaged until she found a torn handkerchief, and hurried downstairs. In a moment Julie was crying in her arms as she searched for the cut, faint, disparaging evidences of which appeared on Julie's dress.

"My thu-umb!" explained Julie. "Oh-h-h-h, t'urts."

"It was the bowl here, the he one," said Hilda apologetically. "It was waitin' on the floor while I polished the sideboard, and Julie come along an' went to foolin' with it. She yust scratch herself."

Evylyn frowned heavily at Hilda, and twisting Julie decisively in her lap, began tearing strips of the handkerchief.

"Now—let's see it, dear."

Julie held it up and Evelyn pounced.

"There!"

Julie surveyed her swathed thumb doubtfully. She crooked it; it waggled. A pleased, interested look appeared in her tear-stained face. She sniffled and waggled it again.

"You precious!" cried Evylyn and kissed her, but before she left the room she levelled another frown at Hilda. Careless! Servants all that way nowadays. If she could get a good Irishwoman—but you couldn't any more—and these Swedes——

At five o'clock Harold arrived and, coming up to her room, threatened in a suspiciously jovial tone to kiss her thirty-five times for her birthday. Evylyn resisted.

"You've been drinking," she said shortly, and then added qualitatively, "a little. You know I loathe the smell of it."

"Evie," he said after a pause, seating himself in a chair by the window, "I can tell you something now. I guess you've known things haven't beep going quite right down-town."

She was standing at the window combing her hair, but at these words she turned and looked at him.

"How do you mean? You've always said there was room for more than one wholesale hardware house in town." Her voice expressed some alarm.

"There was," said Harold significantly, "but this Clarence Ahearn is a smart man."

"I was surprised when you said he was coming to dinner."

"Evie," he went on, with another slap at his knee, "after January first 'The Clarence Ahearn Company' becomes 'The Ahearn, Piper Company'—and 'Piper Brothers' as a company ceases to exist."

Evylyn was startled. The sound of his name in second place was somehow hostile to her; still he appeared jubilant.

"I don't understand, Harold."

"Well, Evie, Ahearn has been fooling around with Marx. If those two had combined we'd have been the little fellow, struggling along, picking up smaller orders, hanging back on risks. It's a question of capital, Evie, and 'Ahearn and Marx' would have had the business just like 'Ahearn and Piper' is going to now." He paused and coughed and a little cloud of whiskey floated up to her nostrils. "Tell you the truth, Evie, I've suspected that Ahearn's wife had something to do with it. Ambitious little lady, I'm told. Guess she knew the Marxes couldn't help her much here."

"Is she—common?" asked Evie.

"Never met her, I'm sure—but I don't doubt it. Clarence Ahearn's name's been up at the Country Club five months—no action taken." He waved his hand disparagingly. "Ahearn and I had lunch together to-day and just about clinched it, so I thought it'd be nice to have him and his wife up to-night—just have nine, mostly family. After all, it's a big thing for me, and of course we'll have to see something of them, Evie."

"Yes," said Evie thoughtfully, "I suppose we will."

Evylyn was not disturbed over the social end of it—but the idea of

"Piper Brothers" becoming "The Ahearn, Piper Company" startled her. It seemed like going down in the world.

Half an hour later, as she began to dress for dinner, she heard his voice from down-stairs.

"Oh, Evie, come down!"

She went out into the hall and called over the banister:

"What is it?"

"I want you to help me make some of that punch before dinner."

Hurriedly rehooking her dress, she descended the stairs and found him grouping the essentials on the dining-room table. She went to the sideboard and, lifting one of the bowls, carried it over.

"Oh, no," he protested, "let's use the big one. There'll be Ahearn and his wife and you and I and Milton, that's five, and Tom and Jessie, that's seven: and your sister and Joe Ambler, that's nine. You don't know how quick that stuff goes when you make it."

"We'll use this bowl," she insisted. "It'll hold plenty. You know how Tom is."

Tom Lowrie, husband to Jessie, Harold's first cousin, was rather inclined to finish anything in a liquid way that he began.

Harold shook his head.

"Don't be foolish. That one holds only about three quarts and there's nine of us, and the servants'll want some—and it isn't strong punch. It's so much more cheerful to have a lot, Evie; we don't have to drink all of it."

"I say the small one."

Again he shook his head obstinately.

"No; be reasonable."

"I am reasonable," she said shortly. "I don't want any drunken men in the house."

"Who said you did?"

"Then use the small bowl."

"Now, Evie——"

He grasped the smaller bowl to lift it back. Instantly her hands were on it, holding it down. There was a momentary struggle, and then, with a little exasperated grunt, he raised his side, slipped it from her fingers, and carried it to the sideboard.

She looked at him and tried to make her expression contemptuous, but he only laughed. Acknowledging her defeat but disclaiming all future interest in the punch, she left the room.

EDGAR ALLAN POE

"Fill with mingled cream and amber,
I will drain that glass again.
Such hilarious visions clamber
Through the chamber of my brain.
Quaintest thoughts—queerest fantasies
Come to life and fade away;
What care I how time advances?
I am drinking ale today."

LIFE IN DEATH

Egli è vivo *e parlerebbe se non osservasse la rigola del silentio.*
INSCRIPTION BENEATH AN ITALIAN PICTURE OF ST. BRUNO.

My fever had been excessive and of long duration. All the remedies attainable in this wild Appennine region had been exhausted to no purpose. My valet and sole attendant in the lonely chateau, was too nervous and too grossly unskillful to venture upon letting blood—of which indeed I had already lost too much in the affray with the banditti. Neither could I safely permit him to leave me in search of assistance. At length I bethought me of a little pacquet of opium which lay with my tobacco in the hookah-case; for at Constantinople I had acquired the habit of smoking the weed with the drug. Pedro handed me the case. I sought and found the narcotic. But when about to cut off a portion I felt the necessity of hesitation. In smoking it was a matter of little importance *how much* was employed. Usually, I had half filled the bowl of the hookah with opium and tobacco cut and mingled intimately, half and half. Sometimes when I had used the whole of this mixture I experienced no very peculiar effects; at other times I would not have smoked the pipe more than two-thirds out, when symptoms of mental derangement, which were even alarming, warned me to desist. But the effect proceeded with an easy gradation which deprived the indulgence of all danger. Here, however, the case was different. I had never *swallowed* opium before. Laudanum and morphine I had occasionally used, and about *them* should have had no reason to hesitate. But the solid drug I had never seen employed. Pedro knew no more respecting the proper quantity to be taken, than myself—and thus, in the sad emergency, I was left altogether to conjecture. Still I felt no especial uneasiness; for I resolved to proceed *by degrees*. I would take a *very* small dose in the first instance. Should this prove impotent, I would repeat it; and so on, until I should find an abatement of the fever, or obtain that sleep which was so pressingly requisite, and with which my reeling senses had not been blessed for now more than a week. No doubt it was this very reeling of my senses—it was the dull delirium which already oppressed me   that prevented me from perceiving the incoherence of my reason—which blinded me to the folly of defining any thing as either large or small where

I had no preconceived standard of comparison. I had not, at the moment, the faintest idea that what I conceived to be an exceedingly small dose of solid opium might, in fact, be an excessively large one. On the contrary I well remember that I judged confidently of the quantity to be taken by reference to the entire quantity of the lump in possession. The portion which, in conclusion, I swallowed, and swallowed without fear, was no doubt a very small proportion *of the piece which I held in my hand.*

The chateau into which Pedro had ventured to make forcible entrance rather than permit me, in my desperately wounded condition, to pass a night in the open air, was one of those fantastic piles of commingled gloom and grandeur which have so long frowned among the Appennines, not less in fact than in the fancy of Mrs. Radcliffe. To all appearance it had been temporarily and very lately abandoned. Day by day we expected the return of the family who tenanted it, when the misadventure which had befallen me would, no doubt, be received as sufficient apology for the intrusion. Meantime, that this intrustion might be taken in better part, we had established ourselves in one of the smallest and least sumptuously furnished apartments. It lay high in a remote turret of the building. Its decorations were rich, yet tattered and antique. Its walls were hung with tapestry and bedecked with manifold and multiform armorial trophies, together with an unusually great number of very spirited modern paintings in frames of rich golden arabesque. In these paintings, which depended from the walls not only in their main surfaces, but in very many nooks which the bizarre architecture of the chateau rendered necessary—in these paintings my incipient delirium, perhaps, had caused me to take deep interest; so that having swallowed the opium, as before told, I bade Pedro to close the heavy shutters of the room—since it was already night—to light the tongues of a tall candelabrum which stood by the head of my bed—and to throw open far and wide the fringed curtains of black velvet which enveloped the bed itself. I wished all this done that I might resign myself, if not to sleep, at least alternately to the contemplation of these pictures, and the perusal of a small volume which had been found upon the pillow, and which purported to criticise and describe them.

Long—long I read—and devoutly, devotedly I gazed. I felt meantime, the voluptuous narcotic stealing its way to my brain. I felt that in its magical influence lay much of the gorgeous richness and variety of the frames—much of the ethereal hue that gleamed from the canvas—and much of the wild interest of the book which I perused. Yet this consciousness rather strengthened than impaired the delight of the illusion, while it weakened the illusion itself. Rapidly and gloriously the hours flew by, and the deep midnight came. The position of the candelabrum displeased me, and outreaching my hand with difficulty, rather than disturb my slumbering valet, I so placed it as to throw its rays more fully upon the book.

But the action produced an effect altogether unanticipated. The rays of the numerous candles (for there were many) now fell within a niche of the room which had hitherto been thrown into deep shade by one of the bed-posts. I thus saw in vivid light a picture all unnoticed before. It was the portrait of a young girl just ripening into womanhood. I glanced at the painting hurriedly, and then closed my eyes. Why I did this was not at first apparent even to my own perception. But while my lids remained thus shut, I ran over in [[my]] mind my reason for so shutting them. It was an impulsive movement to gain time for thought—to make sure that my vision had not deceived me—to calm and subdue my fancy for a more sober and more certain gaze. In a very few moments I again looked fixedly at the painting.

That I now saw aright I could not and would not doubt; for the first flashing of the candles upon that canvas had seemed to dissipate the dreamy stupor which was stealing over my senses, and to startle me into waking life as if with the shock of a galvanic battery.

The portrait, I have already said, was that of a young girl. It was a mere head and shoulders, done in what is technically termed a *vignette* manner; much in the style of the favorite heads of Sully. The arms, the bosom and even the ends of the radiant hair, melted imperceptibly into the vague yet deep shadow which formed the back-ground of the whole. The frame was oval, richly, yet fantastically gilded and filagreed. As a work of art nothing could be more admirable than the painting itself. The loveliness of the face surpassed that of the fabulous Houri. But it could have been neither the execution of the work, nor the immortal beauty of the countenance, which had so suddenly and so vehemently moved me. Least of all, could it have been that my fancy, shaken from its half-slumber, had mistaken the head for that of a living person. I saw at once that the peculiarities of the design, of the *vignetting* and of the frame must have instantly dispelled such idea—must have prevented even its momentary entertainment. Thinking earnestly upon these points, I remained, for some hours perhaps, half sitting, half reclining, with my vision riveted upon the portrait. At length, satisfied of the true secret of its effect, I fell back within the bed. I had found the spell of the picture in a perfect *life-likeliness* of expression, which at first startling, finally confounded, subdued and appalled me. I could no longer support the sad meaning smile of the half-parted lips, nor the too real lustre of the wild eye. With a deep and reverent awe I replaced the candelabrum in its former position. The cause of my deep agitation being thus shut from view, I sought eagerly the volume which discussed the paintings and their histories. Turning to the number which designated the oval portrait, I there read the vague and quaint words which follow:

"She was a maiden of rarest beauty, and not more lovely than full of glee. And evil was the hour when she saw, and loved, and wedded the painter. He, passionate, studious, austere, and having already a bride in his Art: she a maiden of rarest beauty and not more lovely than full of glee: all light and smiles and frolicksome as the young fawn: loving and cherishing all things: hating only the Art which was her rival: dreading only the pallet and brushes and other untoward instruments which deprived her of the countenance of her lover. It was thus a terrible thing for this lady to hear the painter speak of his desire to pourtray even his young bride. But she was humble and obedient and sat meekly for many weeks in the dark high turret-chamber where the light dripped upon the pale canvas only from overhead. But he, the painter, took glory in his work, which went on from hour to hour and from day to day. And he was a passionate, and wild and moody man, who became lost in reveries; so that he *would* not see that the light which fell so ghastlily in that lone turret withered the health and the spirits of his bride, who pined visibly to all but him. Ye [[Yet]] she smiled on and still on, uncomplainingly, because she saw that the painter, (who had high renown,) took a fervid and burning pleasure in his task, and wrought day and night to depict her who so loved him, yet who grew daily more dispirited and weak. And in sooth some who beheld the portrait spoke of its resemblance in low words, as of a mighty marvel and a proof not less of the power of the painter than of his deep love for her whom he depicted so surpassingly well. But at length, as the labor drew nearer to its conclusion, there were admitted none into the turret; for the painter had grown wild with the ardor of his work, and turned his visage from the canvas rarely, even to regard the countenance of his wife. And he *would* not see that the tints which he spread upon the canvas were drawn from the cheeks of her who sate [[sat]] beside him. And when many weeks had passed, and but little remained to do, save one brush upon the mouth and one tint upon the eye, the spirit of the lady again flickered up as the flame within the socket of the lamp. And then the brush was given, and then the tint was placed; and, for one moment, the painter stood entranced before the work which he had wrought; but in the next, while yet he gazed, he grew tremulous and very pallid, and aghast, and crying with a loud voice 'This is indeed *Life* itself!' turned suddenly round to his beloved—*who was dead*. The painter then added—'But is this indeed Death?'"

SPIRITS OF THE DEAD

Thy soul shall find itself alone
'Mid dark thoughts of the gray tombstone
Not one, of all the crowd, to pry
Into thine hour of secrecy.
Be silent in that solitude
Which is not loneliness—for then
The spirits of the dead who stood
In life before thee are again
In death around thee—and their will
Shall overshadow thee: be still.
The night—tho' clear—shall frown—
And the stars shall not look down
From their high thrones in the Heaven,
With light like Hope to mortals given—
But their red orbs, without beam,
To thy weariness shall seem
As a burning and a fever
Which would cling to thee forever.
Now are thoughts thou shalt not banish—
Now are visions ne'er to vanish—
From thy spirit shall they pass
No more—like dew-drops from the grass.
The breeze—the breath of God—is still—
And the mist upon the hill
Shadowy—shadowy—yet unbroken,
Is a symbol and a token—
How it hangs upon the trees,
A mystery of mysteries

A DREAM WITHIN A DREAM

Take this kiss upon the brow!
And, in parting from you now,
Thus much let me avow—
You are not wrong, who deem
That my days have been a dream:
Yet if hope has flown away
In a night, or in a day,
In a vision or in none,
Is it therefore the less *gone?*
All that we see or seem
Is but a dream within a dream.

I stand amid the roar
Of a surf-tormented shore,
And I hold within my hand
Grains of the golden sand—
How few! yet how they creep
Through my fingers to the deep
While I weep—while I weep!
O God! can I not grasp
Them with a tighter clasp?
O God! can I not save
One from the pitiless wave?
Is *all* that we see or seem
But a dream within a dream?

MYSTIFICATION

Slid, if these be your "passados" and "montantes," I'll have none o' them.

NED KNOWLES.

The Baron Ritzner Von Jung was a noble Hungarian family, every member of which (at least as far back into antiquity as any certain records extend) was more or less remarkable for talent of some description—the majority for that species of grotesquerie in conception of which Tieck, a scion of the house, has given a vivid, although by no means the most vivid exemplifications. My acquaintance with Ritzner commenced at the magnificent Chateau Jung, into which a train of droll adventures, not to be made public, threw a place in his regard, and here, with somewhat more difficulty, a partial insight into his mental conformation. In later days this insight grew more clear, as the intimacy which had at first permitted it became more close; and when, after three years of the character of the Baron Ritzner von Jung.

I remember the buzz of curiosity which his advent excited within the college precincts on the night of the twenty-fifth of June. I remember still more distinctly, that while he was pronounced by all parties at first sight "the most remarkable man in the world," no person made any attempt at accounting for his opinion. That he was unique appeared so undeniable, that it was deemed impertinent to inquire wherein the uniquity consisted. But, letting this matter pass for the present, I will merely observe that, from the first moment of his setting foot within the limits of the university, he began to exercise over the habits, manners, persons, purses, and propensities of the whole community which surrounded him, an influence the most extensive and despotic, yet at the same time the most indefinite and altogether unaccountable. Thus the brief period of his residence at the university forms an era in its annals, and is characterized by all classes of people appertaining to it or its dependencies as "that very extraordinary epoch forming the domination of the Baron Ritzner von Jung." then of no particular age, by which I mean that it was impossible to form a guess respecting his age by any data personally afforded. He might have been fifteen or fifty, and was twenty-one years and seven months. He was by no means a handsome man—perhaps the reverse. The contour of his face was somewhat angular and harsh. His forehead was lofty and very fair; his nose a snub; his eyes large, heavy, glassy, and meaningless. About the mouth there was more to be observed. The lips were gently protruded, and rested the one upon the other, after such a fashion that it is impossible to conceive any, even the most complex, combination of human features, conveying so entirely, and so singly, the idea of unmitigated gravity, solemnity and repose.

It will be perceived, no doubt, from what I have already said, that the Baron was one of those human anomalies now and then to be found, who make the science of mystification the study and the business of their lives. For this science a peculiar turn of mind gave him instinctively the cue, while his physical appearance afforded him unusual facilities for carrying his prospects into effect. I quaintly termed the domination of the Baron Ritzner von Jung, ever rightly entered into the mystery which overshadowed his character. I truly think that no person at the university, with the exception of myself, ever suspected him to be capable of a joke, verbal or practical:—the old bull-dog at the garden-gate would sooner have been accused,—the ghost of Heraclitus,—or the wig of the Emeritus Professor of Theology. This, too, when it was evident that the most egregious and unpardonable of all conceivable tricks, whimsicalities and buffooneries were brought about, if not directly by him, at least plainly through his intermediate agency or connivance. The beauty, if I may so call it, of his art mystifique, lay in that consummate ability (resulting from an almost intuitive knowledge of human nature, and a most wonderful self-possession,) by means of which he never failed to make it appear that the drolleries he was occupied in bringing to a point, arose partly in spite, and partly in consequence of the laudable efforts he was making for their prevention, and for the preservation of the good order and dignity of Alma Mater. The deep, the poignant, the overwhelming mortification, which upon each such failure of his praise worthy endeavors, would suffuse every lineament of his countenance, left not the slightest room for doubt of his sincerity in the bosoms of even his most skeptical companions. The adroitness, too, was no less worthy of observation by which he contrived to shift the sense of the grotesque from the creator to the created—from his own person to the absurdities to which he had given rise. In no instance before that of which I speak, have I known the habitual mystific escape the natural consequence of his manoevres—an attachment of the ludicrous to his own character and person. Continually enveloped in an atmosphere of whim, my friend appeared to live only for the severities of society; and not even his own household have for a moment associated other ideas than those of the rigid and august with the memory of the Baron Ritzner von Jung, the demon of the dolce far niente lay like an incubus upon the university. Nothing, at least, was done beyond eating and drinking and making merry. The apartments of the students were converted into so many pot-houses, and there was no pot-house of them all more famous or more frequented than that of the Baron. Our carousals here were many, and boisterous, and long, and never unfruitful of events.

Upon one occasion we had protracted our sitting until nearly daybreak, and an unusual quantity of wine had been drunk. The company consisted of seven or eight individuals besides the Baron and myself. Most of these were young men of wealth, of high connection, of great family pride, and all alive with an exaggerated sense of honor. They abounded in the most ultra German opinions respecting the duello. To these Quixotic notions some recent Parisian publications, backed by three or four desperate and fatal conversation, during the greater part of the night, had run wild upon the all—engrossing topic of the times. The Baron, who had been unusually silent and abstracted in the earlier portion of the evening, at length seemed to be aroused from his apathy, took a leading part in the discourse, and dwelt upon the benefits, and more especially upon the beauties, of the received code of etiquette in passages of arms with an ardor, an eloquence, an impressiveness, and an affectionateness of manner, which elicited the warmest enthusiasm from his hearers in general, and absolutely staggered even myself, who well knew him to be at heart a ridiculer of those very points for which he contended, and especially to hold the entire fanfaronade of duelling etiquette in the sovereign contempt which it deserves.

Looking around me during a pause in the Baron's discourse (of which my readers may gather some faint idea when I say that it bore resemblance to the fervid, chanting, monotonous, yet musical sermonic manner of Coleridge), I perceived symptoms of even more than the general interest in the countenance of one of the party. This gentleman, whom I shall call Hermann, was an original in every respect—except, perhaps, in the single particular that he was a very great fool. He contrived to bear, however, among a particular set at the university, a reputation for deep metaphysical thinking, and, I believe, for some logical talent. As a duellist he had acquired who had fallen at his hands; but they were many. He was a man of courage undoubtedly. But it was upon his minute acquaintance with the etiquette of the duello, and the nicety of his sense of honor, that he most especially prided himself. These things were a hobby which he rode to the death. To Ritzner, ever upon the lookout for the grotesque, his peculiarities had for a long time past afforded food for mystification. Of this, however, I was not aware; although, in the present instance, I saw clearly that something of a whimsical nature was upon the tapis with my friend, and that Hermann was its especial object.

As the former proceeded in his discourse, or rather monologue I perceived the excitement of the latter momently increasing. At length he spoke; offering some objection to a point insisted upon by R., and giving his reasons in detail. To these the Baron replied at length (still maintaining his exaggerated tone of sentiment) and concluding, in what I thought very bad taste, with a sarcasm and a sneer. The hobby of Hermann now took the bit in his teeth. This I could discern by the studied hair-splitting farrago of his rejoinder. His last words I distinctly remember. "Your opinions, allow me to say, Baron von Jung, although in the main correct, are, in many nice points, discreditable to yourself and to the university of which you are a member. In a few respects they are even unworthy of serious refutation. I would say more than this, sir, were it not for the fear of giving you offence (here the speaker smiled blandly), I would say, sir, that your opinions are not the opinions to be expected from a gentleman."

As Hermann completed this equivocal sentence, all eyes were turned upon the Baron. He became pale, then excessively red; then, dropping his pocket-handkerchief, stooped to recover it, when I caught a glimpse of his countenance, while it could be seen by no one else at the table. It was radiant with the quizzical expression which was its natural character, but which I had never seen it assume except when we were alone together, and when he unbent himself freely. In an instant afterward he stood erect, confronting Hermann; and so total an alteration of countenance in so short a period I certainly never saw before. For a moment I even fancied that I had misconceived him, and that he was in sober earnest. He appeared to be stifling with passion, and his face was cadaverously white. For a short time he remained silent, apparently striving to master his emotion. Having at length seemingly succeeded, he reached a decanter which stood near him, saying as he held it firmly clenched "The language you have thought proper to employ, Mynheer Hermann, in addressing yourself to me, is objectionable in so many particulars, that I have neither temper nor time for specification. That my opinions, however, are not the opinions to be expected from a gentleman, is an observation so directly offensive as to allow me but one line of conduct. Some courtesy, nevertheless, is due to the presence of this company, and to yourself, at this moment, as my guest. You will pardon me, therefore, if, upon this consideration, I deviate slightly from the general usage among gentlemen in similar cases of personal affront. You will forgive me for the moderate tax I shall make upon your imagination, and endeavor to consider, for an instant, the reflection of your person in yonder mirror as the living Mynheer Hermann himself.

This being done, there will be no difficulty whatever. I shall discharge this decanter of wine at your image in yonder mirror, and thus fulfil all the spirit, if not the exact letter, of resentment for your insult, while the necessity of physical violence to your real person will be obviated."

With these words he hurled the decanter, full of wine, against the mirror which hung directly opposite Hermann; striking the reflection of his person with great precision, and of course shattering the glass into fragments. The whole company at once started to their feet, and, with the exception of myself and Ritzner, took their departure. As Hermann went out, the Baron whispered me that I should follow him and make an offer of my services. To this I agreed; not knowing precisely what to make of so ridiculous a piece of business.

The duellist accepted my aid with his stiff and ultra recherche air, and, taking my arm, led me to his apartment. I could hardly forbear laughing in his face while he proceeded to discuss, with the profoundest gravity, what he termed "the refinedly peculiar character" of the insult he had received. After a tiresome harangue in his ordinary style, he took down from his book shelves a number of musty volumes on the subject of the duello, and entertained me for a long time with their contents; reading aloud, and commenting earnestly as he read. I can just remember the titles of some of the works. There were the "Ordonnance of Philip le Bel on Single Combat"; the "Theatre of Honor," by Favyn, and a treatise "On the Permission of Duels," by Andiguier. He displayed, also, with much pomposity, Brantome's "Memoirs of Duels,"—published at Cologne, 1666, in the types of Elzevir—a precious and unique vellum-paper volume, with a fine margin, and bound by Derome. But he requested my attention particularly, and with an air of mysterious sagacity, to a thick octavo, written in barbarous Latin by one Hedelin, a Frenchman, and having the quaint title, "Duelli Lex Scripta, et non; aliterque." From this he read me one of the drollest chapters in the world concerning "Injuriae per applicationem, per constructionem, et per se," about half of which, he averred, was strictly applicable to his own "refinedly peculiar" case, although not one syllable of the whole matter could I understand for the life of me. Having finished the chapter, he closed the book, and demanded what I thought necessary to be done. I replied that I had entire confidence in his superior delicacy of feeling, and would abide by what he proposed. With this answer he seemed flattered, and sat down to write a note to the Baron. It ran thus:

Sir,—My friend, M. P.-, will hand you this note. I find it incumbent upon me to request, at your earliest convenience, an explanation of this evening's occurrences at your chambers. In the event of your declining this request, Mr. P. will be happy to arrange, with any friend whom you may appoint, the steps preliminary to a meeting.

With sentiments of perfect respect,

Your most humble servant,

JOHANN HERMAN.

To the Baron Ritzner von Jung,

Not knowing what better to do, I called upon Ritzner with this epistle. He bowed as I presented it; then, with a grave countenance, motioned me to a seat. Having perused the cartel, he wrote the following reply, which I carried to Hermann.

SIR,—Through our common friend, Mr. P., I have received your note of this evening. Upon due reflection I frankly admit the propriety of the explanation you suggest. This being admitted, I still find great difficulty, (owing to the refinedly peculiar nature of our disagreement, and of the personal affront offered on my part,) in so wording what I have to say by way of apology, as to meet all the minute exigencies, and all the variable shadows, of the case. I have great reliance, however, on that extreme delicacy of discrimination, in matters appertaining to the rules of etiquette, for which you have been so long and so pre-eminently distinguished. With perfect certainty, therefore, of being comprehended, I beg leave, in lieu of offering any sentiments of my own, to refer you to the opinions of Sieur Hedelin, as set forth in the ninth paragraph of the chapter of "Injuriae per applicationem, per constructionem, et per se," in his "Duelli Lex scripta, et non; aliterque." The nicety of your discernment in all the matters here treated, will be sufficient, I am assured, to convince you that the mere circumstance of me referring you to this admirable passage, ought to satisfy your request, as a man of honor, for explanation.

With sentiments of profound respect,

Your most obedient servant,

VON JUNG.

The Herr Johann Hermann

Hermann commenced the perusal of this epistle with a scowl, which, however, was converted into a smile of the most ludicrous self-complacency as he came to the rigmarole about Injuriae per applicationem, per constructionem, et per se. Having finished reading, he begged me, with the blandest of all possible smiles, to be seated, while he made reference to the treatise in question. Turning to the passage specified, he read it with great care to himself, then closed the book, and desired me, in my character of confidential acquaintance, to express to the Baron von Jung his exalted sense of his chivalrous behavior, and, in that of second, to assure him that the explanation offered was of the fullest, the most honorable, and the most unequivocally satisfactory nature.

Somewhat amazed at all this, I made my retreat to the Baron. He seemed to receive Hermann's amicable letter as a matter of course, and after a few words of general conversation, went to an inner room and brought out the everlasting treatise "Duelli Lex scripta, et non; aliterque." He handed me the volume and asked me to look over some portion of it. I did so, but to little purpose, not being able to gather the least particle of meaning. He then took the book himself, and read me a chapter aloud. To my surprise, what he read proved to be a most horribly absurd account of a duel between two baboons. He now explained the mystery; showing that the volume, as it appeared prima facie, was written upon the plan of the nonsense verses of Du Bartas; that is to say, the language was ingeniously framed so as to present to the ear all the outward signs of intelligibility, and even of profundity, while in fact not a shadow of meaning existed. The key to the whole was found in leaving out every second and third word alternately, when there appeared a series of ludicrous quizzes upon a single combat as practised in modern times.

The Baron afterwards informed me that he had purposely thrown the treatise in Hermann's way two or three weeks before the adventure, and that he was satisfied, from the general tenor of his conversation, that he had studied it with the deepest attention, and firmly believed it to be a work of unusual merit. Upon this hint he proceeded. Hermann would have died a thousand deaths rather than acknowledge his inability to understand anything and everything in the universe that had ever been written about the duello.

JAMES JOYCE

*"The light music of whiskey
falling into a glass—an agreeable interlude."*

JAMES JOYCE

GAS FROM A BURNER

Ladies and gents, you are here assembled
To hear why earth and heaven trembled
Because of the black and sinister arts
Of an Irish writer in foreign parts.
He sent me a book ten years ago
I read it a hundred times or so
Backwards and forwards, down and up,
Through both the ends of a telescope.
I printed it all to the very last word
But by the mercy of the Lord
The darkness of my mind was rent
And I saw the writer's foul intent.
But I owe a duty to Ireland:
I held her honour in my hand,
This lovely land that always sent
Her writers and artists to banishment
And in a spirit of Irish fun
Betrayed her own leaders, one by one.
'Twas Irish humour, wet and dry,
Flung quicklime into Parnell's eye;
'Tis Irish brains that save from doom
The leaky barge of the Bishop of Rome
For everyone knows the Pope can't belch
Without the consent of Billy Walsh.
O Ireland my first and only love
Where Christ and Caesar are hand and glove!
O lovely land where the shamrock grows!
(Allow me, ladies, to blow my nose)
To show you for strictures I don't care a button
I printed the poems of Mountainy Mutton
And a play he wrote (you've read it I'm sure)
Where they talk of *bastard*, *bugger* and *whore*
And a play on the Word and Holy Paul
And some woman's legs that I can't recall

Written by Moore, a genuine gent
That lives on his property's ten per cent:
I printed mystical books in dozens:
I printed the table-book of Cousins
Though (asking your pardon) as for the verse
'Twould give you a heartburn on your arse:
I printed folklore from North and South
By Gregory of the Golden Mouth:
I printed poets, sad, silly and solemn:
I printed Patrick What-do-you-Colm:
I printed the great John Milicent Synge
Who soars above on an angel's wing
In the playboy shift that he pinched as swag
From Maunsel's manager's travelling-bag.
But I draw the line at that bloody fellow
That was over here dressed in Austrian yellow,
Spouting Italian by the hour
To O'Leary Curtis and John Wyse Power
And writing of Dublin, dirty and dear,
In a manner no blackamoor printer could bear.
Shite and onions! Do you think I'll print
The name of the Wellington Monument,
Sydney Parade and Sandymount tram,
Downes's cakeshop and Williams's jam?
I'm damned if I do--I'm damned to blazes!
Talk about *Irish Names of Places!*
It's a wonder to me, upon my soul,
He forgot to mention Curly's Hole.
No, ladies, my press shall have no share in
So gross a libel on Stepmother Erin.
I pity the poor--that's why I took
A red-headed Scotchman to keep my book.
Poor sister Scotland! Her doom is fell;
She cannot find any more Stuarts to sell.
My conscience is fine as Chinese silk:
My heart is as soft as buttermilk.
Colm can tell you I made a rebate
Of one hundred pounds on the estimate
I gave him for his Irish Review.
I love my country--by herrings I do!
I wish you could see what tears I weep

When I think of the emigrant train and ship.
That's why I publish far and wide
My quite illegible railway guide,
In the porch of my printing institute
The poor and deserving prostitute
Plays every night at catch-as-catch-can
With her tight-breeched British artilleryman
And the foreigner learns the gift of the gab
From the drunken draggletail Dublin drab.
Who was it said: Resist not evil?
I'll burn that book, so help me devil.
I'll sing a psalm as I watch it burn
And the ashes I'll keep in a one-handled urn.
I'll penance do with farts and groans
Kneeling upon my marrowbones.
This very next lent I will unbare
My penitent buttocks to the air
And sobbing beside my printing press
My awful sin I will confess.
My Irish foreman from Bannockburn
Shall dip his right hand in the urn
And sign crisscross with reverent thumb
Memento homo upon my bum.

DUBLINERS: A LITTLE CLOUD

Eight years before he had seen his friend off at the North Wall and wished him godspeed. Gallaher had got on. You could tell that at once by his travelled air, his well-cut tweed suit, and fearless accent. Few fellows had talents like his and fewer still could remain unspoiled by such success. Gallaher's heart was in the right place and he had deserved to win. It was something to have a friend like that.

Little Chandler's thoughts ever since lunch-time had been of his meeting with Gallaher, of Gallaher's invitation and of the great city London where Gallaher lived. He was called Little Chandler because, though he was but slightly under the average stature, he gave one the idea of being a little man. His hands were white and small, his frame was fragile, his voice was quiet and his manners were refined. He took the greatest care of his fair silken hair and moustache and used perfume discreetly on his handkerchief. The half-moons of his nails were perfect and when he smiled you caught a glimpse of a row of childish white teeth.

As he sat at his desk in the King's Inns he thought what changes those eight years had brought. The friend whom he had known under a shabby and necessitous guise had become a brilliant figure on the London Press. He turned often from his tiresome writing to gaze out of the office window. The glow of a late autumn sunset covered the grass plots and walks. It cast a shower of kindly golden dust on the untidy nurses and decrepit old men who drowsed on the benches; it flickered upon all the moving figures—on the children who ran screaming along the gravel paths and on everyone who passed through the gardens. He watched the scene and thought of life; and (as always happened when he thought of life) he became sad. A gentle melancholy took possession of him. He felt how useless it was to struggle against fortune, this being the burden of wisdom which the ages had bequeathed to him.

He remembered the books of poetry upon his shelves at home. He had bought them in his bachelor days and many an evening, as he sat in the little room off the hall, he had been tempted to take one down from the bookshelf and read out something to his wife. But shyness had always held him back; and so the books had remained on their shelves. At times he repeated lines to himself and this consoled him.

When his hour had struck he stood up and took leave of his desk and of his fellow-clerks punctiliously. He emerged from under the feudal arch of the King's Inns, a neat modest figure, and walked swiftly down Henrietta Street. The golden sunset was waning and the air had grown sharp. A horde of grimy children populated the street. They stood or ran in the roadway or crawled up the steps before the gaping doors or squatted like mice upon the thresholds. Little Chandler gave them no thought. He picked his way deftly through all that minute vermin-like life and under the shadow of the gaunt spectral mansions in which the old nobility of Dublin had roystered. No memory of the past touched him, for his mind was full of a present joy.

He had never been in Corless's but he knew the value of the name. He knew that people went there after the theatre to eat oysters and drink liqueurs; and he had heard that the waiters there spoke French and German. Walking swiftly by at night he had seen cabs drawn up before the door and richly dressed ladies, escorted by cavaliers, alight and enter quickly. They wore noisy dresses and many wraps. Their faces were powdered and they caught up their dresses, when they touched earth, like alarmed Atalantas. He had always passed without turning his head to look. It was his habit to walk swiftly in the street even by day and whenever he found himself in the city late at night he hurried on his way apprehensively and excitedly. Sometimes, however, he courted the causes of his fear. He chose the darkest and narrowest streets and, as he walked boldly forward, the silence that was spread about his footsteps troubled him, the wandering silent figures troubled him; and at times a sound of low fugitive laughter made him tremble like a leaf.

He turned to the right towards Capel Street. Ignatius Gallaher on the London Press! Who would have thought it possible eight years before? Still, now that he reviewed the past, Little Chandler could remember many signs of future greatness in his friend. People used to say that Ignatius Gallaher was wild. Of course, he did mix with a rakish set of fellows at that time, drank freely and borrowed money on all sides. In the end he had got mixed up in some shady affair, some money transaction: at least, that was one version of his flight. But nobody denied him talent. There was always a certain ... something in Ignatius Gallaher that impressed you in spite of yourself. Even when he was out at elbows and at his wits' end for money he kept up a bold face. Little Chandler remembered (and the remembrance brought a slight flush of pride to his cheek) one of Ignatius Gallaher's sayings when he was in a tight corner:

"Half time now, boys," he used to say light-heartedly. "Where's my considering cap?"

That was Ignatius Gallaher all out; and, damn it, you couldn't but admire him for it.

Little Chandler quickened his pace. For the first time in his life he felt himself superior to the people he passed. For the first time his soul revolted against the dull inelegance of Capel Street. There was no doubt about it: if you wanted to succeed you had to go away. You could do nothing in Dublin. As he crossed Grattan Bridge he looked down the river towards the lower quays and pitied the poor stunted houses. They seemed to him a band of tramps, huddled together along the riverbanks, their old coats covered with dust and soot, stupefied by the panorama of sunset and waiting for the first chill of night bid them arise, shake themselves and begone. He wondered whether he could write a poem to express his idea. Perhaps Gallaher might be able to get it into some London paper for him. Could he write something original? He was not sure what idea he wished to express but the thought that a poetic moment had touched him took life within him like an infant hope. He stepped onward bravely.

Every step brought him nearer to London, farther from his own sober inartistic life. A light began to tremble on the horizon of his mind. He was not so old—thirty-two. His temperament might be said to be just at the point of maturity. There were so many different moods and impressions that he wished to express in verse. He felt them within him. He tried to weigh his soul to see if it was a poet's soul. Melancholy was the dominant note of his temperament, he thought, but it was a melancholy tempered by recurrences of faith and resignation and simple joy. If he could give expression to it in a book of poems perhaps men would listen. He would never be popular: he saw that. He could not sway the crowd but he might appeal to a little circle of kindred minds. The English critics, perhaps, would recognise him as one of the Celtic school by reason of the melancholy tone of his poems; besides that, he would put in allusions. He began to invent sentences and phrases from the notice which his book would get. *"Mr Chandler has the gift of easy and graceful verse."* ... *"A wistful sadness pervades these poems."* ... *"The Celtic note."* It was a pity his name was not more Irish-looking. Perhaps it would be better to insert his mother's name before the surname: Thomas Malone Chandler, or better still: T. Malone Chandler. He would speak to Gallaher about it.

He pursued his revery so ardently that he passed his street and had to turn back. As he came near Corless's his former agitation began to overmaster him and he halted before the door in indecision. Finally he opened the door and entered.

The light and noise of the bar held him at the doorways for a few moments. He looked about him, but his sight was confused by the shining of many red and green wine-glasses The bar seemed to him to be full of people and he felt that the people were observing him curiously. He glanced quickly to right and left (frowning slightly to make his errand appear serious), but when his sight cleared a little he saw that nobody had turned to look at him: and there, sure enough, was Ignatius Gallaher leaning with his back against the counter and his feet planted far apart.

"Hallo, Tommy, old hero, here you are! What is it to be? What will you have? I'm taking whisky: better stuff than we get across the water. Soda? Lithia? No mineral? I'm the same. Spoils the flavour.... Here, *garçon*, bring us two halves of malt whisky, like a good fellow.... Well, and how have you been pulling along since I saw you last? Dear God, how old we're getting! Do you see any signs of aging in me—eh, what? A little grey and thin on the top—what?"

Ignatius Gallaher took off his hat and displayed a large closely cropped head. His face was heavy, pale and clean-shaven. His eyes, which were of bluish slate-colour, relieved his unhealthy pallor and shone out plainly above the vivid orange tie he wore. Between these rival features the lips appeared very long and shapeless and colourless. He bent his head and felt with two sympathetic fingers the thin hair at the crown. Little Chandler shook his head as a denial. Ignatius Galaher put on his hat again.

"It pulls you down," he said. "Press life. Always hurry and scurry, looking for copy and sometimes not finding it: and then, always to have something new in your stuff. Damn proofs and printers, I say, for a few days. I'm deuced glad, I can tell you, to get back to the old country. Does a fellow good, a bit of a holiday. I feel a ton better since I landed again in dear dirty Dublin.... Here you are, Tommy. Water? Say when."

Little Chandler allowed his whisky to be very much diluted.

"You don't know what's good for you, my boy," said Ignatius Gallaher. "I drink mine neat."

"I drink very little as a rule," said Little Chandler modestly. "An odd half-one or so when I meet any of the old crowd: that's all."

"Ah, well," said Ignatius Gallaher, cheerfully, "here's to us and to old times and old acquaintance."

They clinked glasses and drank the toast.

"I met some of the old gang today," said Ignatius Gallaher. "O'Hara seems to be in a bad way. What's he doing?"

"Nothing," said Little Chandler. "He's gone to the dogs."

"But Hogan has a good sit, hasn't he?"

"Yes; he's in the Land Commission."

"I met him one night in London and he seemed to be very flush.... Poor O'Hara! Boose, I suppose?"

"Other things, too," said Little Chandler shortly.

Ignatius Gallaher laughed.

"Tommy," he said, "I see you haven't changed an atom. You're the very same serious person that used to lecture me on Sunday mornings when I had a sore head and a fur on my tongue. You'd want to knock about a bit in the world. Have you never been anywhere even for a trip?"

"I've been to the Isle of Man," said Little Chandler.

Ignatius Gallaher laughed.

"The Isle of Man!" he said. "Go to London or Paris: Paris, for choice. That'd do you good."

"Have you seen Paris?"

"I should think I have! I've knocked about there a little."

"And is it really so beautiful as they say?" asked Little Chandler.

He sipped a little of his drink while Ignatius Gallaher finished his boldly.

"Beautiful?" said Ignatius Gallaher, pausing on the word and on the flavour of his drink. "It's not so beautiful, you know. Of course, it is beautiful.... But it's the life of Paris; that's the thing. Ah, there's no city like Paris for gaiety, movement, excitement...."

Little Chandler finished his whisky and, after some trouble, succeeded in catching the barman's eye. He ordered the same again.

"I've been to the Moulin Rouge," Ignatius Gallaher continued when the barman had removed their glasses, "and I've been to all the Bohemian cafés. Hot stuff! Not for a pious chap like you, Tommy."

Little Chandler said nothing until the barman returned with two glasses: then he touched his friend's glass lightly and reciprocated the former toast. He was beginning to feel somewhat disillusioned. Gallaher's accent and way of expressing himself did not please him. There was something vulgar in his friend which he had not observed before. But perhaps it was only the result of living in London amid the bustle and competition of the Press. The old personal charm was still there under this new gaudy manner. And, after all, Gallaher had lived, he had seen the world. Little Chandler looked at his friend enviously.

"Everything in Paris is gay," said Ignatius Gallaher. "They believe in enjoying life—and don't you think they're right? If you want to enjoy yourself properly you must go to Paris. And, mind you, they've a great feeling for the Irish there. When they heard I was from Ireland they were ready to eat me, man."

Little Chandler took four or five sips from his glass.

"Tell me," he said, "is it true that Paris is so ... immoral as they say?"

Ignatius Gallaher made a catholic gesture with his right arm.

"Every place is immoral," he said. "Of course you do find spicy bits in Paris. Go to one of the students' balls, for instance. That's lively, if you like, when the *cocottes* begin to let themselves loose. You know what they are, I suppose?"

"I've heard of them," said Little Chandler.

Ignatius Gallaher drank off his whisky and shook his head.

"Ah," he said, "you may say what you like. There's no woman like the Parisienne—for style, for go."

"Then it is an immoral city," said Little Chandler, with timid insistence—"I mean, compared with London or Dublin?"

"London!" said Ignatius Gallaher. "It's six of one and half-a-dozen of the other. You ask Hogan, my boy. I showed him a bit about London when he was over there. He'd open your eye.... I say, Tommy, don't make punch of that whisky: liquor up."

"No, really...."

"O, come on, another one won't do you any harm. What is it? The same again, I suppose?"

"Well ... all right."

"*François*, the same again.... Will you smoke, Tommy?"

Ignatius Gallaher produced his cigar-case. The two friends lit their cigars and puffed at them in silence until their drinks were served.

"I'll tell you my opinion," said Ignatius Gallaher, emerging after some time from the clouds of smoke in which he had taken refuge, "it's a rum world. Talk of immorality! I've heard of cases—what am I saying?—I've known them: cases of ... immorality...."

Ignatius Gallaher puffed thoughtfully at his cigar and then, in a calm historian's tone, he proceeded to sketch for his friend some pictures of the corruption which was rife abroad. He summarised the vices of many capitals and seemed inclined to award the palm to Berlin. Some things he could not vouch for (his friends had told him), but of others he had had personal experience. He spared neither rank nor caste. He revealed many of the secrets of religious houses on the Continent and described some of the practices which were fashionable in high society and ended by telling, with details, a story about an English duchess—a story which he knew to be true. Little Chandler was astonished.

"Ah, well," said Ignatius Gallaher, "here we are in old jog-along Dublin where nothing is known of such things."

"How dull you must find it," said Little Chandler, "after all the other places you've seen!"

"Well," said Ignatius Gallaher, "it's a relaxation to come over here, you know. And, after all, it's the old country, as they say, isn't it? You can't help having a certain feeling for it. That's human nature.... But tell me something about yourself. Hogan told me you had ... tasted the joys of connubial bliss. Two years ago, wasn't it?"

Little Chandler blushed and smiled.

"Yes," he said. "I was married last May twelve months."

"I hope it's not too late in the day to offer my best wishes," said Ignatius Gallaher. "I didn't know your address or I'd have done so at the time."

He extended his hand, which Little Chandler took.

"Well, Tommy," he said, "I wish you and yours every joy in life, old chap, and tons of money, and may you never die till I shoot you. And that's the wish of a sincere friend, an old friend. You know that?"

"I know that," said Little Chandler.

"Any youngsters?" said Ignatius Gallaher.

Little Chandler blushed again.

"We have one child," he said.

"Son or daughter?"

"A little boy."

Ignatius Gallaher slapped his friend sonorously on the back.

"Bravo," he said, "I wouldn't doubt you, Tommy."

Little Chandler smiled, looked confusedly at his glass and bit his lower lip with three childishly white front teeth.

"I hope you'll spend an evening with us," he said, "before you go back. My wife will be delighted to meet you. We can have a little music and———"

"Thanks awfully, old chap," said Ignatius Gallaher, "I'm sorry we didn't meet earlier. But I must leave tomorrow night."

"Tonight, perhaps...?"

"I'm awfully sorry, old man. You see I'm over here with another fellow, clever young chap he is too, and we arranged to go to a little card-party. Only for that...."

"O, in that case...."

"But who knows?" said Ignatius Gallaher considerately. "Next year I may take a little skip over here now that I've broken the ice. It's only a pleasure deferred."

"Very well," said Little Chandler, "the next time you come we must have an evening together. That's agreed now, isn't it?"

"Yes, that's agreed," said Ignatius Gallaher. "Next year if I come, *parole d'honneur.*"

"And to clinch the bargain," said Little Chandler, "we'll just have one more now."

Ignatius Gallaher took out a large gold watch and looked at it.

"Is it to be the last?" he said. "Because you know, I have an a.p."

"O, yes, positively," said Little Chandler.

"Very well, then," said Ignatius Gallaher, "let us have another one as a *deoc an doruis*—that's good vernacular for a small whisky, I believe."

Little Chandler ordered the drinks. The blush which had risen to his face a few moments before was establishing itself. A trifle made him blush at any time: and now he felt warm and excited. Three small whiskies had gone to his head and Gallaher's strong cigar had confused his mind, for he was a delicate and abstinent person. The adventure of meeting Gallaher after eight years, of finding himself with Gallaher in Corless's surrounded by lights and noise, of listening to Gallaher's stories and of sharing for a brief space Gallaher's vagrant and triumphant life, upset the equipoise of his sensitive nature. He felt acutely the contrast between his own life and his friend's and it seemed to him unjust. Gallaher was his inferior in birth and education. He was sure that he could do something better than his friend had ever done, or could ever do, something higher than mere tawdry journalism if he only got the chance. What was it that stood in his way? His unfortunate timidity! He wished to vindicate himself in some way, to assert his manhood. He saw behind Gallaher's refusal of his invitation. Gallaher was only patronising him by his friendliness just as he was patronising Ireland by his visit.

The barman brought their drinks. Little Chandler pushed one glass towards his friend and took up the other boldly.

"Who knows?" he said, as they lifted their glasses. "When you come next year I may have the pleasure of wishing long life and happiness to Mr and Mrs Ignatius Gallaher."

Ignatius Gallaher in the act of drinking closed one eye expressively over the rim of his glass. When he had drunk he smacked his lips decisively, set down his glass and said:

"No blooming fear of that, my boy. I'm going to have my fling first and see a bit of life and the world before I put my head in the sack—if I ever do."

"Some day you will," said Little Chandler calmly.

Ignatius Gallaher turned his orange tie and slate-blue eyes full upon his friend.

"You think so?" he said.

"You'll put your head in the sack," repeated Little Chandler stoutly, "like everyone else if you can find the girl."

He had slightly emphasised his tone and he was aware that he had betrayed himself; but, though the colour had heightened in his cheek, he did not flinch from his friend's gaze. Ignatius Gallaher watched him for a few moments and then said:

"If ever it occurs, you may bet your bottom dollar there'll be no mooning and spooning about it. I mean to marry money. She'll have a good fat account at the bank or she won't do for me."

Little Chandler shook his head.

"Why, man alive," said Ignatius Gallaher, vehemently, "do you know what it is? I've only to say the word and tomorrow I can have the woman and the cash. You don't believe it? Well, I know it. There are hundreds—what am I saying?—thousands of rich Germans and Jews, rotten with money, that'd only be too glad.... You wait a while my boy. See if I don't play my cards properly. When I go about a thing I mean business, I tell you. You just wait."

He tossed his glass to his mouth, finished his drink and laughed loudly. Then he looked thoughtfully before him and said in a calmer tone:

"But I'm in no hurry. They can wait. I don't fancy tying myself up to one woman, you know."

He imitated with his mouth the act of tasting and made a wry face.

"Must get a bit stale, I should think," he said.

THE HOLY OFFICE

Myself unto myself will give
This name, Katharsis Purgative.
I, who dishevelled ways forsook
To hold the poet's grammar book,
Bringing to tavern and to brothel
The mind of witty Aristotle
Lest bards in the attempt should err
Must here be my interpreter.
Wherefore receive now from my lip
Peripatetic scholarship.
To enter heaven, travel hell,
Be piteous or terrible
One positively needs the ease
Of plenary indulgences.
For every true born mysticist
A Dante is, unprejudiced,
Who safe at inglenook, by proxy,
Hazards extremes of heterodoxy,
Like him who finds joy at a table
Pondering the uncomfortable.
Ruling one's life by commonsense
How can one fail to be intense?
But I must not accounted be
One of that mumming company
With him who hies him to appease
His giddy dames' frivolities
While they console him when he whinges
With gold-embroidered Celtic fringes
Or him who sober all the day
Mixes a naggin in his play
Or him whose conduct 'seems to own'
His preference for a man of 'tone'
Or him who plays the ragged patch
To millionaires in Hazelpatch

But weeping after holy fast
Confesses all his pagan past
Or him who will his hat unfix
Neither to malt nor crucifix
But show all that poor-dressed be
His high Castillian courtesy
Or him who loves his Master dear
Or him who drinks his pint in fear
Or him who once when snug abed
Saw Jesus Christ without his head
And tried so hard to win for us
The long-lost works of Aeschylus.
But all these men of whom I speak
Make me the sewer of their clique.
That they may dream their dreamy dreams
I carry off their filthy streams
For I can do these things for them
Through which I lost my diadem,
Those things for which Grandmother Church
Left me severely in the lurch.
Thus I relieve their timid arses,
Perform my office of Katharsis.
My scarlet leaves them white as wool.
Through me they purge a bellyful.
To sister mummers one and all
I act as vicar-general
And for each maiden, shy and nervous,
I do a similar kind of service.
For I detect without surprise
The shadowy beauty in her eyes,
The 'dare not' of sweet maidenhood
That answers my corruptive 'would,'
Whenever publicly we meet
She never seems to think of it.
At night when close in bed she lies
And feels my hand between her thighs
My little love in light attire
Knows the soft flame of desire.
But Mammon places under ban
The uses of Leviathan
And that high spirit ever wars

On Mammon's countless servitors
Nor can they ever be exempt
From his taxation of contempt.
So distantly I turn to view
The shamblings of that motley crew,
Those souls that hate the strength that mine has
Steeled in the school of old Aquinas.
Where they have crouched and crawled and prayed
I stand, the self-doomed, unafraid,
Unfellowed, friendless and alone,
Indifferent as the herring bone,
Firm as the mountain ridges where
I flash my antlers on the air.
Let them continue as is meet
To adequate the balance sheet.
Though they may labour to the grave
My spirit they shall never have
Nor make my soul with theirs as one
Till the Mahamanvatara be done.
And though they spurn me at their door
My soul shall spurn them evermore.

O. HENRY

*"Turn up the lights.
I don't want to go home in the dark."*

THE MURDERER

"I push my boat among the reeds;
I sit and stare about;
Queer slimy things crawl through the weeds,
Put to a sullen rout.
I paddle under cypress trees;
All fearfully I peer
Through oozy channels when the breeze
Comes rustling at my ear.

"The long moss hangs perpetually;
Gray scalps of buried years;
Blue crabs steal out and stare at me,
And seem to gauge my fears;
I start to hear the eel swim by;
I shudder when the crane
Strikes at his prey; I turn to fly
At drops of sudden rain.

"In every little cry of bird
I hear a tracking shout;
From every sodden leaf that's stirred
I see a face frown out;
My soul shakes when the water rat
Cowed by the blue snake flies;
Black knots from tree holes glimmer at
Me with accusive eyes.

"Through all the murky silence rings
A cry not born of earth;
And endless, deep, unechoing thing
That owns not human birth,
I see no colors in the sky
Save red, as blood is red;
I pray to God to still that cry
From pallid lips and dead.

"One spot in all that stagnant waste
I shun as moles shun light,
And turn my prow to make all haste
To fly before the night.
A poisonous mound hid from the sun,
Where crabs hold revelry;
Where eels and fishes feed upon
The Thing that once was He.

"At night I steal along the shore;
Within my hut I creep;
But awful stars blink through the door,
To hold me from my sleep.
The river gurgles like his throat,
In little choking coves,
And loudly dins that phantom note
From out the awful groves.

"I shout with laughter through the night:
I rage in greatest glee;
My fears all vanish with the light
Oh! splendid nights they be!
I see her weep; she calls his name;
He answers not, nor will;
My soul with joy is all aflame;
I laugh, and laugh, and thrill.

"I count her teardrops as they fall;
I flout my daytime fears;
I mumble thanks to God for all
These gibes and happy jeers.
But, when the warning dawn awakes,
Begins my wandering;
With stealthy strokes through tangled brakes,
A wasted, frightened thing."

NOTHING TO SAY

"You can tell your paper," the great man said,
"I refused an interview.
I have nothing to say on the question, sir;
Nothing to say to you."

And then he talked till the sun went down
And the chickens went to roost;
And he seized the collar of the poor young man,
And never his hold he loosed.

And the sun went down and the moon came up,
And he talked till the dawn of day;
Though he said, "On this subject mentioned by you,
I have nothing whatever to say."

And down the reporter dropped to sleep
And flat on the floor he lay;
And the last he heard was the great man's words,
"I have nothing at all to say."

DROP A TEAR IN THIS SLOT

He who, when torrid Summer's sickly glare
Beat down upon the city's parched walls,
Sat him within a room scarce 8 by 9,
And, with tongue hanging out and panting breath,
Perspiring, pierced by pangs of prickly heat,
Wrote variations of the seaside joke
We all do know and always loved so well,
And of cool breezes and sweet girls that lay
In shady nooks, and pleasant windy coves
Anon
Will in that self-same room, with tattered quilt
Wrapped round him, and blue stiffening hands,
All shivering, fireless, pinched by winter's blasts,
Will hale us forth upon the rounds once more,
So that we may expect it not in vain,
The joke of how with curses deep and coarse
Papa puts up the pipe of parlor stove.
So ye
Who greet with tears this olden favorite,
Drop one for him who, though he strives to please
Must write about the things he never sees.

OSCAR WILDE was an Irish novelist, poet, essayist and playwright who became one of London's most popular playwrights at the peak of his career. Following his classics-heavy education, Wilde developed and focused his writing on the emerging Aesthetic Movement of the late 19th century.

Some of Wilde's most famous work includes his sole novel, *The Picture of Dorian Gray*, his play, *The Importance of Being Earnest*, and a letter written while he was in prison, *De Profundis*. In addition to his fame from his writing career, Wilde was known for his witty and flamboyant personality and fashion.

However, Wilde's career took a dark turn in 1895 when he was charged with sodomy and gross indecency for stories of his romantic relationships with men. After being charged as guilty, Wilde was convicted and sentenced to two years' hard labor. This time in prison cost greatly on the writer's health and emotional wellbeing.

Although he continued to write after his release from prison, Wilde's health continued to decline and he developed an addiction to alcohol, specifically absinthe. He spent the last three years of his life in exile and poverty. He died on November 30, 1990 at the age of 46 from a case of meningitis.

DOROTHY PARKER, known as Dottie or Dot during her life, was born Dorothy Rothschild in New Jersey August 22, 1893. Her education ended when she was 14, and her mother, step mother, uncle, and father all died by the time she was 20.

Parker contributed works to Vogue, Vanity Fair, The New Yorker and Life. She worked as a poet, short story writer, and critic. She published her first short story in 1922 and won the O. Henry award for her piece Big Blonde in 1929. She was married twice, screen writing for companies such as MGM and Paramount with her second husband. During the 1920s, Parker travel to Europe several times and befriended fellow authors such as Ernest Hemingway and F. Scott Fitzgerald. She was also known as a strong feminist.

It was known that Parker suffered from alcoholism and depression. She attempted suicide several times.

Despite the sadness she experienced in life, Parker excelled at composing the humor in every day events. After she died from a heart attack at age 73, the New York Times describe Parker in her obituary as "the sardonic humorist who purveyed her wit in conversation, short stories, verse and criticism."

F. SCOTT FITZGERALD was born September 24, 1896 in St. Paul, Minnesota to Mary "Molly" McQuillan—an Irish immigrant—and Edward Fitzgerald—a failed wicker furniture salesman.

Fitzgerald was encouraged to pursue writing after his detective stories were published in the high school newspaper. He published his first book, "This Side of Paradise," in 1920. Fitzgerald had started the novel while studying at Princeton, but dropped out to join the Army in World War I. While stationed near Montgomery, Alabama, Fitzgerald met the woman who would become his wife.

Zelda, described as a "freethinking woman with the world at her disposal" provided inspiration for much of her husband's work. At 27 years old, Zelda suffered her first mental breakdown, initiated by nervous exhaustion due to intense work in pursuit of becoming a professional ballerina. She was eventually diagnosed with schizophrenia and sought treatment in and out of clinics until she died.

Zelda's illness had a debilitating effect on her husband and his writing. When Fitzgerald published his next novel several years later, it was commercially unsuccessful and worsened his developing drinking problem.

While working as a scriptwriter in Hollywood, he fell in love with a famous gossip columnist and, "for the rest of his life – except for occasional drunken spells when he became bitter and violent – Fitzgerald lived quietly with her."

He died of a heart attack at 44 years old, with his final novel left unfinished.

EDGAR ALLAN POE was born in Boston, Massachusetts on January 19, 1809. Poe was an orphan by the age of three and became a foster child in Richmond, Virginia to John and Frances Allan. Poe was well educated and went to the University of Virginia. However, he was forced to leave because of extreme gambling debts.

He was enlisted in the United States Army for a short time, after which he published his first collection of poems, Tamerlane and Other Poems. He moved to Baltimore, Maryland to live with his aunt and cousin soon after.

Poe sold short stories to magazines and became the editor of the Southern Literary Messenger. He also married his 14-year-old cousin, Virginia. He lost his wife to tuberculosis at the young age of 24. It is said that Poe's alcoholism surpassed his limits, especially after the death of so many loved ones.

Edgar Allan Poe went on to publish many short stories, including The Raven and The Tell-Tale Heart, all of which eluded to a dark and twisted way of thinking.

His death is nothing short of mystery, similar to his stories, and his cause of death is still unknown. Many ideas are discussed by critics to this day, but one main assumption is alcohol poisoning.

JAMES JOYCE was born February 2, 1882 in Dublin, Ireland. As a child, Joyce expressed a strong passion for literature and was encouraged by his family to obtain a highbrow Jesuit education. Joyce later attended University College, Dublin where he earned a Bachelor of Arts degree in 1902. A year after his graduation, Joyce began traveling around Europe working odd jobs to fuel his writing.

In 1920 Joyce settled in Paris until World War II when he escaped to Zurich, Switzerland. He spent the rest of his life in Switzerland.

Joyce's writings show his famous, stream-of-consciousness writing style. This technique of writing generates a sense that the readers are listening to the character's thoughts. His use of satire and humor is prominent through all his writings and portrays hidden messages. Joyce used these techniques to develop his own style defined by subtly and naturalism.

In his early years, Joyce struggled to be published. His choice of complex and explicit content caused bans on his writing in many countries including the United Kingdom and United States. Joyce once said, "If Ulysses' isn't fit to read, life isn't fit to live."

Joyce lived most of his life as a functioning alcoholic. He credited alcohol for helping him write his famous novel Ulysses, believing himself not to write as effectively when sober.

Despite his modest beginnings and alcoholic tendencies, James Joyce continued to produce work until his death in Switzerland at age 58 in 1941.

O. HENRY was born William Sydney Porter on September 11, 1862 in Greensboro, North Carolina. O. Henry had many different careers throughout his life. He started as a clerk in a drugstore before he moved to Texas and worked on a ranch. He then worked in a general land office and later as a teller for a bank. Around 1887, O. Henry started writing and later wrote for the Houston Post.

In 1896, O. Henry was indicted for embezzlement of bank funds and fled to Honduras. When he learned his wife was deathly sick, he came back to the states and was taken to prison in Columbus, Ohio after her death. During his three years in prison, O. Henry wrote stories for magazines to offer his daughter financial support. It was here O. Henry adopted his pseudonym.

O. Henry moved to New York in 1902. He wrote a story a week for the New York World and also wrote for magazines. Although he was very popular with his readers, O. Henry struggled financially and suffered from alcoholism. He died on June 5, 1910.

APPENDIX

Beckson, Karl. "Ocsar Wilde." *Encyclopaedia Britannica*. October 17, 2016. https://www.britannica.com/biography/Oscar-Wilde.

Biography.com Editors. "James Joyce Biography." *The Biography.com website*. Feburary 3, 2016. October 17, 2016. http://www.biography.com/people/james-joyce-9358676.

————Biography.com Editors. "Oscar Wilde Biography." *The Biography.com website*. April 2, 2014. October 17, 2016. http://www.biography.com/people/oscar-wilde-9531078#video-gallery.

————Biography.com Editors. "William Sydney Porter Biography." *The Biography.com website*. April 2, 2014. October 17, 2016. http://www.biography.com/people/william-sydney-porter-9542046#profile.

"Biography of James Joyce." *The Literature Network*. October 17,2016. http://www.online-literature.com/james_joyce/.

Brdnik, Gregory. "Oscar Wilde Biography." *Oscar Wilde Online*. June 27, 2015. October 17, 2016. http://www.wilde-online.info/oscar-wilde-biography.htm.

"Biography." *Dorothy Parker Society*. October 17, 2016. http://www.dorothyparker.com/wordpress/biography.

———— "New York Times Obituary." *Dorothy Parker Society*. October 17, 2016. http://www.dorothyparker.com/wordpress/gallery/new-york-times-obituary.

"Edgar Allan Poe." *Academy of American Poets*. October 17,2016. https://www.poets.org/poetsorg/poet/edgar-allan-poe.

Editors of Encyclopaedia Britannica. "O.Henry." *Encycolpaedia Britannica*. October 17, 2016. https://www.britannica.com/biography/O-Henry.

Fitzgerald, F. Scott. "The Beautiful and the Damned Book Three." *Project Gutenburg*. October 17, 2016. http://www.gutenburg.org/ebooks/9830?msg=welcome_stranger.

————Fitzgerald, F. Scott. "The Cut-Glass Bowl." *Project Gutenburg*. October 17, 2016. http://www.gutenberg.org/files/4368/4368-h/4368-h.htm#The_Cut-Glass_Bowl.

APPENDIX

————Fitzgerald, F. Scott. "Jemina, The Mountain Girl." *Project Gutenburg.* October 17, 2015. http://www.gutenberg.org/cache/epub/6695/pg6695-images.html.

Henry, O. "Drop a Tear in This Slot." *Google Books.* October 17, 2016. https://books.google.com/books?id=ZkZDAQAAMAAJ&pg=PA825&lpg=PA825&dq=nothing+to+say+o+henry&source=bl&ots=zx7w7RryIJ&sig=4BbWFvtv_pljXmZ337G ANXUsR-Q&hl=en&sa=X&ved=0ahUKEwjcwqKpt4_PAhWEbT4KHfBFAOIQ6AEIOjAF#v=onepage&q=nothing%20to%20say%20o%20henry&f=false.

————Henry, O. "Nothing to Say." *Google Books.* October 17, 2016. https://books.google.com/books?id=ZkZDAQAAMAAJ&pg=PA825&lpg=PA825&dq=nothing+to+say+o+henry&source=bl&ots=zx7w7RryIJ&sig=4BbWFvtv_pljXmZ337G ANXUsR-Q&hl=en&sa=X&ved=0ahUKEwjcwqKpt4_PAhWEbT4KHfBFAOIQ6AEIOjAF#v=onepage&q=nothing%20to%20say%20o%20henry&f=false.

————Henry, O. "The Murderer." *Google Books.* October 17, 2016. https://books.google.com/books?id=ZkZDAQAAMAAJ&pg=PA825&lpg=PA825&dq=nothing+to+say+o+henry&source=bl&ots=zx7w7RryIJ&sig=4BbWFvtv_pljXmZ337G ANXUsR-Q&hl=en&sa=X&ved=0ahUKEwjcwqKpt4_PAhWEbT4KHfBFAOIQ6AEIOjAF#v=onepage&q=nothing%20to%20say%20o%20henry&f=false.

Joyce, James. "Dubliners; A Little Cloud." *Project Gutenburg.* October 17, 2016. https://www.gutenberg.org/files/2814/2814-h/2814-h.htm.

————Joyce, James. "Gas from a Burner." *Genius Media Group Inc.* October 17, 2016. http://genius.com/James-joyce-gas-from-a-burner-annotated.

————Joyce, James. "The Holy Office." *Blue Ridge Journal.* October 17, 2016. http://www.blueridgejournal.com/poems/jj-holy.htm.

Menand, Louis. "Silence, Exile, Punning: James Joyce's chance encounters." *The New Yorker.* July 2, 2012. October 17, 2016. http://www.newyorker.com/magazine/2012/07/02/silence-exile-punning.

Mizener, Arthur. "F. Scott Fitzgerald." *Encyclopaedia Britannica.* October 17, 2016. https://www.britannica.com/biography/F-Scott-Fitzgerald.

"Dorothy Parker." *New World Encyclopedia.* March 25, 2015. OCtober 17, 2016. http://www.newworldencyclopedia.org/entry/Dorothy_Parker.

Parker, Dorothy. "Men: A Hate Song." *Vanity Fair.* August 30, 2103. October 17, 2016. http://www.vanityfair.com/news/1917/02/dorothy-parker-hate-song-men.

————Parker, Dorothy. "Reformers: A Hymn of Hate." *Project Gutenburg.* October 17, 2016. https://www.gutenberg.org/files/6678/6678-h/6678-h.htm.

APPENDIX

————Parker, Dorothy. "Such a Pretty Little Picture." *Dotonline*. October 17, 2016. http://dotonline. pbworks.com/w/page/18130594/Such%20A%20Pretty%20Little%20Picture.

Photograph of Dorothy Parker. *Wikimedia Commons*. October 17, 2016. https://commons.wikimedia. org/wiki/Category:Dorothy_Parker#/media/File:Young_Dorothy_Parker.jpg.

Photograph of Edgar Allan Poe. *Wikimedia Commons*. October 17, 2016. https://en.wikipedia.org/ wiki/File:Edgar_Allan_Poe_2.jpg.

Photograph of F. Scott Fitzgerald. *Wikimedia Commons*. Ocober 17, 2016. https://commons. wikimedia.org/wiki/F._Scott_Fitzgerald#/media/File:F_Scott_Fitzgerald_1921.jpg.

Photograph of James Joyce. *Wikipedia*. October 17, 2016. https://en.wikipedia.org/wiki/James_ Joyce.

Photograph of O. Henry. *Find A Grave*. October 17, 2016. http://www.findagrave.com/cgi-bin/ fg.cgi?page=pv&GRid=772&PIpi=387601.

Photograph of Oscar Wilde. *Wikimedia Commons*. October 17, 2016. https://commons.wikimedia. org/wiki/File:Oscar_Wilde_portrait.jpg.

Poe, Edgar Allan. "A Dream Within a Dream." *Project Gutenburg*. October 17, 2016. http://www. gutenberg.org/files/10031/10031-h/10031-h.htm#section5l.

————Poe, Edgar Allan. "Spirits of the Dead." *Project Gutenbrug*. October 17, 2016. http://www. gutenberg.org/files/10031/10031-h/10031-h.htm#section5.

"Poe's Life." *Poe Museum*. October 17, 2016. https://www.poemuseum.org/life.php.

"F. Scott Fitzgerald." *Simon & Schuster*. October 17, 2016. http://www.simonandschuster.com/ authors/F-Scott-Fitzgerald/698896.

Wilde, Oscar. "Panthea." *The Literature Netwrok*. October 17, 2016. http://www.online-literature. com/wilde/2277/

————Wilde, Oscar. "Preface to The Picture of Dorian Gray." *Project Gutenburg*. October 17, 2016. http://www.gutenberg.org/files/174/174-h/174-h.htm.

Willet, Erika. "F. Scott Fitzgerald and the American Dream." *PBS*. October 17, 2016. http://www. pbs.org/kteh/amstorytellers/bios.html.